Academic Writing Now

Academic Writing Now

NOW WITH
MLA 2016
UPDATES

A Brief Guide for Busy Students

DAVID STARKEY

broadview press

BROADVIEW PRESS – www.broadviewpress.com
Peterborough, Ontario, Canada

Founded in 1985, Broadview Press remains a wholly independent publishing house. Broadview's focus is on academic publishing; our titles are accessible to university and college students as well as scholars and general readers. With over 600 titles in print, Broadview has become a leading international publisher in the humanities, with world-wide distribution. Broadview is committed to environmentally responsible publishing and fair business practices.

The interior of this book is printed on 100% recycled paper.

PERMANENT   100%

© 2017 David Starkey

Library and Archives Canada Cataloguing in Publication

Starkey, David, 1962-, author
      Academic writing now : a brief guide for busy students / David Starkey.

"Now with MLA 2016 updates."
Includes bibliographical references and index.
ISBN 978-1-55481-380-3 (softcover)

      1. Academic writing. I. Title.

LB2369.S73 2017   808'.02   C2017-901388-2

Broadview Press handles its own distribution in North America
PO Box 1243, Peterborough, Ontario K9J 7H5, Canada
555 Riverwalk Parkway, Tonawanda, NY 14150, USA
Tel: (705) 743-8990; Fax: (705) 743-8353
email: customerservice@broadviewpress.com

Distribution is handled by Eurospan Group in the UK, Europe, Central Asia, Middle East, Africa, India, Southeast Asia, Central America, South America, and the Caribbean. Distribution is handled by Footprint Books in Australia and New Zealand.

Broadview Press acknowledges the financial support of the Government of Canada through the Canada Book Fund for our publishing activities.

Edited by Martin R. Boyne

Book design by Chris Rowat Design

PRINTED IN CANADA

For Sandy

&

for my students,
who taught me everything I know

A stitch in time saves nine.
—*English Proverb*

Contents

Preface for Instructors: Busy, Busy, Busy

As you prepare to skim over this preface, you are, no doubt, very busy. In addition to the class or classes you're teaching (and the countless essays you're grading), you may have numerous departmental responsibilities. Possibly you're also writing and publishing your own work. And most of us have personal lives that are at least as complex as those we reveal to the public.

Of course, if *you* feel overwhelmed, your students probably feel the time crunch even more. In addition to taking classes, many are working and— let's face it—probably enjoying some of the freedoms and privileges that come with adulthood.

Time, for all of us, is in short supply.

Enter *Academic Writing Now: A Brief Guide for Busy Students*, a rhetoric designed to cover the basics of a college writing course in a concise, student-friendly format.

While the book can be successfully used in any first-year writing course, what distinguishes it from others in a crowded market is the fact that it is written by a community-college English professor for two- and four-year college and university instructors who, like the author, are in the trenches, facing the same set of challenges—multiple course sections, oversized rosters, heavy paper loads—week after week, month after month, year after year.

While some of our more fortunate senior colleagues may teach a single composition class a year, just to keep their hand in, most of us don't have the luxury of spending hours sifting through a mammoth tome looking for the perfect assignment. Like our students, we're always ready to cut to the chase. Unfortunately, most composition textbooks labeled "brief rhetorics" contain hundreds of pages that are, strictly speaking, unnecessary. *Academic Writing Now* assumes students will read the entire book; therefore, anything inessential to the business of college writing has been excluded. Each chapter concentrates on a crucial element of composing an academic essay and is capable of being read in a single sitting. The book is loaded with "timesaver tips," ideas for making the most of the student's time, along with occasional warnings to avoid errors frequently made by student writers. Each short chapter concludes with questions and suggestions designed to trigger class discussion.

In addition to explaining how to navigate the demands of academic writing, the book's chief aim is to engage students at the conversational level we try to establish in our classrooms. The prose is student-friendly, but on point and goal-driven. *Academic Writing Now* makes the reasonable assumption that most students would rather be doing something else besides reading a composition textbook.

But what, exactly, should students be learning? Many of our colleagues in American high schools are now teaching to the Common Core State Standards for English Language Arts & Literacy. That's quite a mouthful, but what it boils down to is writing instruction that is "(1) research and evidence based, (2) aligned with college and work expectations, (3) rigorous, and (4) internationally benchmarked."

For better or worse—depending on whom you're talking to—college instructors typically have more leeway in their courses than high-school teachers. Nevertheless, the general goals of the Common Core are probably not too far from your own. Most of us must follow a course of study outline approved by a curriculum committee. Our departments and institutions require students to learn summary and paraphrase, thesis and argument. Our students analyze texts and argue positions. They must write persuasive, evidence-based research papers. Learning to master these skills in as little time as ten weeks means focusing intently on the reading and writing process itself rather than on memorizing a broad spectrum of facts.

As a result, you won't find any sections here on, say, logical fallacies, and we'll only briefly touch on common grammar errors. Instructors can direct students to plenty of free and excellent publisher- and university-sponsored websites covering this material (Purdue University's Online Writing Lab, or OWL, is exemplary). Similarly, the book's few complete essays are used to illustrate the basics of academic writing. Excellent and inexpensive readers abound, and many English instructors have begun assigning the many first-rate—and free—readings available online.

Ultimately, *Academic Writing Now* acknowledges that much of the learning in any writing course takes place in the interaction between students and their teachers, classmates, tutors, family, and friends. A good textbook is crucial, but it's only part of the picture. This one errs on the side of leaving the kitchen sink in the kitchen, where it belongs.

Introduction for Students: Strategies for Succeeding as a College Writer

Students arrive at their college or university with different goals and backgrounds, but the one thing you almost certainly have in common with everyone else on campus is a sense that there's not enough time in the day (or night) to accomplish everything you want to do.

Academic Writing Now: A Brief Guide for Busy Students is designed to save you time by 1) concisely explaining how to compose an academic essay, and 2) conveying that information in a friendly, conversational fashion. In short, I hope you'll want to read this book because it tells you what you need to know and because it is enjoyable to read—at least as enjoyable as a textbook can be.

Throughout the book, I'll address ways to make your life as a busy college student slightly less hectic. Often these will be small tips I've culled not just from my 25 years of teaching composition classes, but from scouring the work of my fellow academics and reading some of the many books and articles by time-management specialists. Let's begin, though, with some overall student-success strategies that you can use for just about every assignment in every course you take.

Prioritize

Time-management consultants tell us that above all we must learn to prioritize—to decide which task needs doing first and when. Every day of the semester, you'll need, accurately and honestly, to assess what must be completed *first*.

Imagine that tomorrow you have a quiz in history that's worth only 5 per cent of your overall grade. You also have an essay in your English class that accounts for 20 per cent of your total points. Even if you prefer history to English, your real focus must be on the English paper—it's one-fifth of your entire grade. Therefore, though you might spend up to an hour studying for the quiz, you'll need to use the rest of the time working on your essay.

Prioritizing in college is really just a matter of deciding on the *urgency* and *importance* of any particular assignment. In a perfect world, you would be able to give every assignment its proper due, and if you have plenty of free study time, you may come close to making that happen. However, most students face occasions when an activity they consider lacking in urgency has to give way to something more important.

Set Achievable Goals

The majority of decisions about prioritizing are far less clear-cut than the history quiz vs. English essay example described above. Fortunately, one of the best tactics for prioritizing is also one of the simplest: making to-do lists, often in the form of daily schedules. Once you see what you *must* do, you'll be able to set realistic and achievable goals.

Let's say it's Tuesday, and your first essay is due next Monday. Let's also say that you haven't done anything so far, so it's time to get moving. Suppose the essay assignment requires you to analyze and respond to a single article. You might divide your work as follows:

- *Tuesday*: Read and annotate article
- *Wednesday*: Summarize article, write double-entry journal, generate initial thesis and outline
- *Thursday*: Study for math test on Friday morning (no time to work on Essay)
- *Friday*: Write as much of essay #1 as possible (plan on ending by 5 p.m. for social time)
- *Saturday*: Complete first draft of essay #1, study for anthropology exam
- *Sunday*: Revise essay, study for anthro, do a final proofreading of essay before going to bed
- *Monday*: Turn in essay #1

You'll notice that while this schedule is far from perfect, it is at least realistic. It takes into account the fact that the important assignments due in two other classes, which I've grayed out, will take some time away from your writing process. The schedule also acknowledges that college isn't all work: you need to set aside some time for fun.

That said, the schedule also recognizes that a week is probably the minimum amount of time the average writer needs to complete a passable final draft. Can you really write a *good* essay in two hours? Maybe. Wouldn't it be much better if you took the entire two or three weeks you've been given, breaking the process into many short segments? Of course it would.

Setting achievable goals means avoiding procrastination. You may think you're procrastinating because your best work happens in a pinch, but more likely you're either afraid of failing, or you're one of those perfectionists who can't stand even the tiniest defect in their own work. However, as I'll emphasize throughout this book, it's okay to fail—in moderation, and especially in the early stages of the writing process where even professional writers often encounter difficulties. Writing professor Donald Murray told his classes, "Great is the enemy of good." Murray wasn't suggesting that students not *strive* for greatness, but he wanted them to be realistic, to realize there were times when it was better to settle for simply being proficient.

Perfection comes at a high price, especially in writing, where nothing is ever really perfect. Samuel Beckett famously said, "Try again. Fail again. Fail better." Part of becoming a successful college student involves admitting you will fail occasionally. Over time, you will identify your strengths and weaknesses, cultivating the former and reducing the latter. Indeed, Arthur Costa and Bena Kallick, in their fascinating book *Habits of Mind*, note that applying past knowledge to new situations is one of the keys to achievement in any field.

Reward Yourself for Achieving Your Goals

Some people are capable of writing an entire first draft in a single go. Others have trouble completing a paragraph before feeling in dire need of a break. Most of us prefer to have at least a quiet hour or two to work on a writing project, and those periods of composition can be quite exhausting.

Writing can be gratifying in its own right, but it's still important to give yourself a little something extra for completing the work you set out to do. It might be ten minutes of texting with friends, or a quick nap, or a run around campus, or a close yet *short* encounter with your favorite video game. It doesn't matter what the reward is, just as long as you feel you'll be compensated for your labor.

Stephen R. Covey, author of *The 7 Habits of Highly Effective People*, calls this necessary mental and physical renewal "sharpening the saw," and he believes "it is the habit that makes all the others possible." Fiction writer Richard Ford even advises, "Try turning on the TV. That always works for me. I forget all about writing the second *SportsCenter* comes on."

On the other hand, make sure the rewards you allot yourself aren't greater than the amount of effort you've actually expended. I love to play music, for instance, and my writing room is crowded with musical instruments:

acoustic and electric guitars, basses, a drum kit, a keyboard, a mandolin. When I face a difficult passage in a writing assignment, temptation is all around me. It's so much more fun to strike up a tune than it is to revise a paragraph that doesn't quite make sense.

And yet I've learned over the years that if I give in to these temptations, it will only prolong what I have to do, and I won't enjoy the music nearly as much as I would have if I'd postponed it as a reward for completing my work.

It's similar to having a long drive ahead of you: while you may need to pull over occasionally to stretch and take care of your basic needs, if you do so every time you get bored, you'll never make your way home. In short, thirty minutes of television for every ten minutes of writing won't result in a whole lot of productivity.

Slotting these reward breaks into your writing schedule is yet another reason to avoid procrastination. If it's midnight and your paper is due at eight the next morning, there won't be much time for double-fudge sundaes.

Minimize Distractions

If you've recently moved from home into college housing, you may worry about how you're ever going to get your writing done. Noise, parties, new friends dropping by all the time, distractions galore: what's a student to do?

Finding a space in which to study is one of the most common problems faced by college students. If you're in a dorm or apartment and have your own room, close the door. If not, you'll need to try and schedule quiet time with your roommate or roommates. That isn't always possible, of course, so you may end up deciding to write in the campus library, or in a coffee shop, or outside, if the weather's nice.

Students who attend college and live at home have probably already identified good times and places to study. Take advantage of those periods when no one is going to bother you.

Wherever you live, you'll want to identify habits that distract you from your work—for example, constantly checking your phone or email or social-media pages. If you're having trouble settling into a reading and writing groove, you may even need to take the drastic step of disconnecting yourself from the wired world. If you write on a computer or tablet but keep getting sidetracked by online enticements, you may want to disable your Internet connection as you type, and turning off your phone while you compose an essay is nearly always a good idea. Chapter 3 covers invention strategies—ways to get started when you're feeling blocked—but a good first step is simply to give yourself some peace and quiet.

Say "No"

The best way to minimize distractions is to just say "no." Sure, that party down the hall sounds like a lot of fun, but it will probably still be going on after you get back from the library, and you'll feel much better about joining in the festivities knowing you've completed your assigned writing task for the day.

Temporary distractions are relatively easy to resist. However, if you're putting yourself through college, it may be harder to tell your boss that you can't work Sunday because you have to turn in your essay on Monday. You may have to compromise sometimes, but remember those difficult refusals now will, in years to come, allow you more frequently to say "yes" to the things you really want to do.

Ask for Help

Talking about a writing assignment to anyone is a good idea, although your instructor will normally be your go-to option. The easiest way to ask him or her is simply to raise your hand in class, but if you don't feel comfortable doing that, all instructors keep office hours, and many will be willing to answer brief questions via email.

Chances are your campus also has a writing center. Often the tutors are well-trained fellow students, which usually makes for a cordial and productive conference.

Finally, the casual conversations you have with friends, family, and classmates can be as worthwhile as anything that takes place in a more formal environment. Say, for instance, you've been assigned to write about whether or not the legal drinking age should be lowered from 21 to 18. Your parents, worried about your safety, may have one perspective, while your older brother may feel very differently, and the exchange student from Italy may have something else entirely to contribute.

Remind Yourself of Why You're Here

Some students come to college with the exclusive goal of learning. They want to know everything, and they look at every class as a potential windfall of wisdom and vitality. If you're one of those students, congratulations, you're already ahead of the game.

Most students, however, enter college with the idea that it is an important part of a much longer journey. They aspire to interesting careers. They imagine the financial success that will help support themselves and their families, including the parents whose hard work has helped get them where they are.

During those gloomy hours when you feel your essay will never come together, or when your assigned reading seems to have been composed in Martian, visualize yourself completing your immediate task, and then project further into the future. Ultimately, the mental picture you want to hang onto is yourself in a cap and gown, receiving your diploma and going out into the working world armed with confidence and the lasting skills you'll learn in a class such as this one.

"Keep your eyes on the prize," civil rights leaders reminded people pushing for justice and equality in the second half of the twentieth century. They had big dreams, and they accomplished many of them. You can, too.

PART ONE: READY, SET...

CHAPTER ONE

Academic Writing: An Overview

WHY WRITE?
WRITING AS INQUIRY AND PROCESS
HIGH-SCHOOL VS. UNIVERSITY ENGLISH
WHAT DO PROFESSORS *REALLY* WANT?

WHY WRITE?

When we're not clear on the goals others assign for us, we sometimes procrastinate or refuse to engage in the assigned tasks at all. In order to maximize the time you spend on your composition class, it's helpful to think about what's involved in academic writing and why your instructor believes it's necessary for you to learn the skills taught in this class. As you settle into your academic term, you may be wondering, "Why do I have to take a composition class in the first place?"

There are plenty of answers to that question. The most practical one is that many of the courses you enroll in as an undergraduate—even if you are majoring in the natural sciences or computer science or engineering— will require some writing, and many majors insist on quite a lot of writing. Refining this talent is crucial to your success in higher education.

Later, once you enter the working world, you'll find that writing well makes you an invaluable worker or employer. Companies of all sizes frequently cite the ability to communicate well as an employee's biggest asset. Therefore, knowing how to write clearly and persuasively is one of the most portable skills you can take away from your college education.

Learning to write well also means cultivating *critical thinking*, a habit of mind that seeks truth by taking nothing for granted. Critical thinking leads to thoughtful and productive participation in our democracy. Most everyone feels strongly about at least one social issue, whether it's gun control or voting rights or which books should be in the local school library.

However, unless you are able to articulate the reasons behind your beliefs, you're unlikely to convince others to follow them.

In short, writing well is one of the most useful skills you will learn as an undergraduate. Mastering the writing process isn't always easy, but it is never a waste of your time.

WRITING AS INQUIRY AND PROCESS

Writing instructors often use the term "writing as inquiry," and another reason for learning to write well is to discover your own core values. We write to find out what we still need to know, to learn where our beliefs connect with other people's and where they differ. "Start with questions, not answers," writing professor Bruce Ballenger advises, and this book heartily endorses that belief. Without questions, we never get to the answers.

The act of inquiry is usually a multi-step procedure, so it's not surprising if you often hear your instructor talking about the "writing process" as though it were a fact of life, like the Second Law of Thermodynamics, or Jay Z. I've already used the phrase several times in this book—what does it mean?

Basically, we English teachers believe that very little writing can't be improved by returning to it again and again. Yes, sometimes you only have two hours to write a midterm or final examination, but in college writing classes the assumption is that an out-of-class essay will go through more than one draft. For ease of explanation, textbooks tend to break writing into various steps, and *Academic Writing Now* is no different. That's why the book is divided into three main sections: "Ready, Set...," "Go," and "Go Again." The racing metaphor is in keeping with the book's focus on making efficient use of your time, but writing well rarely resembles a hundred-meter dash. In fact, writing a strong academic essay is probably more like taking an afternoon walk in the woods. Still, even the most leisurely walker must ultimately reach a destination, and when the woods are thick and the sun is going down, it helps to have a map. *Academic Writing Now* is that map.

Breaking down the writing process allows for a fuller discussion of each step in composing an academic essay, though of course you already know that when you're in the midst of writing, you're likely to be juggling all sorts of mental processes. While you're jotting down one idea, another idea occurs to you that belongs somewhere else in your essay. After you write the second idea, you realize the sentence that follows it needs to be rephrased, so you might jump from what we call invention to revision in just a matter of seconds. While students generally find it useful to think of writing as a multi-step process, there's no denying that the way many of us actually write can be awfully messy. Acknowledging that fact, composition theorists use the word **recursive** to signal the importance of repeating the various stages of the process, in whatever order they happen to occur.

HIGH-SCHOOL VS. UNIVERSITY ENGLISH

You've been learning to write for years now, and high-school English classes are crucial to your development as a writer. Nevertheless, part of entering a college writing class is shedding habits that helped you succeed in high school but may hurt you now.

For instance, if your high-school experience validated the idea that the longest papers with the biggest words get the best grades, you'll probably be disappointed in college. Most university writing instructors prefer a voice closer to the one you actually speak with than the made-up one you may have used in your previous essays. You don't want to sound like you're just hanging out with your friends, but it's important to present yourself as a real-life human being, not a thesaurus gone haywire.

It's not only the tone and diction of your essays you'll need to consider modifying, but also their structure. Just about every American high-school student is familiar with the five-paragraph theme: introduction, three body paragraphs, conclusion. It's a useful contraption, helping to keep the student focused and allowing an overworked instructor to quickly assess whether or not the essay is on target.

However, many college instructors find the format too restrictive. They're concerned that students won't delve deep into an issue if they're always worried about finding three main points. Sometimes there's only one main point, but it needs to be explored in depth. Other times, you may have four or five important shorter ideas that you want to convey in your essay.

In general, you'll find that college assignments allow you more freedom to explore your ideas, but they also require that you think about your topic much more thoroughly. Below are three examples of the types of "prompts," or writing assignments, you might encounter in a college composition course:

- After reading an article that maintains that racism is still prevalent in North America, use outside research as well as your own experience to explain the extent to which you agree or disagree with the article. Use the personal pronoun "I" whenever necessary.
- Read two articles with contrasting positions on the importance of competitive football and basketball programs to the overall financial and spiritual health of universities. Decide which article best summarizes your own opinion and explain why.

- Research what you consider to be a pressing social problem. Identify the causes, determine the current effects, and propose at least one feasible solution.

Assignments like these will oblige you to have a thorough understanding of the articles and books you discuss, which is why the next chapter is devoted to polishing your reading skills. You'll notice also that the topics are relatively open-ended. You're not asked to take a definitive position, but rather to "explain the extent to which you agree or disagree" and determine "which article best summarizes your own opinion."

One of the pleasures—maybe we should we say *shocks*—of receiving a college education is learning how many contrasting opinions there are on any given topic. For many students, the take-away from their first year of university is just how large and complicated the world really is.

WHAT DO PROFESSORS *REALLY* WANT?

Several years ago, the administrators at my college asked me to develop a Writing Across the Curriculum handbook. I spent the academic year talking to colleagues, holding workshops, and collecting written responses to a questionnaire from every department on campus.

Three pieces of advice emerged again and again. My fellow professors wanted students to 1) be clear, 2) address their audience, and 3) stay on task. Based on my research, I'd say those goals are widely held in the United States and Canada, and I think most students can reasonably hope to achieve them by the end of an academic term—as long as they work hard and make effective use of their instructor's expertise and campus resources.

While essay writing may seem daunting at the beginning of the term, once you get into the swing of things, you'll find it gets easier. Fortunately, as I suggested earlier, there's no "wasted" writing. Suppose you finish typing your first draft and decide you hate it. Even if you Select All and hit the Delete key, you've still gained valuable practice in crafting sentences, organizing paragraphs, and thinking on the page.

Finally, remember that most composition instructors are pretty generous people. If they'd been intent on making a fortune, they would have gone into hedge-fund management. Instead, they are passionate about writing and learning; they want their students to succeed. This means that even if you haven't written academic essays recently, your instructor will be pulling for you. Your teacher knows that as the term progresses, your papers will get better. They really will.

Timesaver Tip: Accept the fact you will not enjoy every writing assignment. Professors assign essays to help their students learn, and it's the rare professor who deliberately asks for an essay that he or she thinks students will hate writing. Nevertheless, you will inevitably receive assignments that you don't want to do. You can spend hours, or even days, moaning and groaning about what a waste of time writing the essay will be. Of course, the real waste of time is complaining about a required assignment. The quicker you face what you need to do, the sooner it will be done.

Questions and Suggestions FOR You

1. Write a short "literacy narrative" in which you describe your own history as a writer. Begin with the first time you remember putting words on paper or a computer screen and go all the way to the present. Questions 2–7 might be incorporated into this narrative, or your instructor may ask you to answer them separately.

2. What's the most important thing you've ever written and why?

3. What are your biggest challenges as a writer? If English is not your native language, what difficulties have you faced writing in a second (or third or fourth or fifth) language?

4. Who do you write for most frequently? Teachers, friends, family, yourself? How does your personal writing differ from your writing for school?

5. What issues are most likely to interfere with your writing this term? Make a list, and then brainstorm a possible solution for each potential problem.

6. List all the places where you write: in your room, in class, on the bus, etc. Then jot down how well you write in each location, and which places will be most conducive to the academic writing you'll be doing in this class. Go to those safe places whenever you can.

7. This chapter emphasizes the belief, widely held among college writing instructors, that writing is a *process*. To what extent has your own writing experience been based on process? That is, how often have you revised an essay multiple times, with each draft evolving from the previous one? In contrast, how likely are you to concentrate on quickly producing a single, standardized "product"?

Questions and Suggestions FROM You

List three questions you still have after reading this chapter. If reviewing the chapter doesn't inspire three questions, think about the overall topic of "academic writing." What don't you know about the subject that you would really like to know?

1. _____

_____

_____

_____

_____

2. _____

_____

_____

_____

3. _____

_____

_____

_____

_____

Building on past successes is a sure way to continue them in the future. Therefore, each chapter in *Academic Writing Now* ends with a request that you jot down an activity *not mentioned in the chapter* that you have done in previous classes and that might be helpful for you and other students in your current class.

For Chapter 1, describe *one* activity related to academic writing that you think would be helpful to do in class. It could be a Q & A session with your instructor, a debate on some aspect of academic writing, a freewriting exercise, a list of your academic writing fears or triumphs, etc. Any successful activity you've been part of in any course you've ever taken might serve as a model.

_____

_____

_____

_____

_____

CHAPTER TWO

Academic Reading

EFFECTIVE READING HABITS
ANNOTATION
DOUBLE-ENTRY JOURNAL
ANALYSIS
SUMMARY
REVERSE OUTLINE
PARAPHRASE
QUOTATIONS

EFFECTIVE READING HABITS

The Need to Read

A student once told me he had a confession to make. I prepared myself for the worst—a crime he'd committed, or a tragedy in his family—but he simply wanted me to know that reading wasn't exactly his favorite thing to do.

That student was far from alone. Sure, most students do a lot of *informal* reading: if you're writing texts and email messages and online posts, you're reading them, too. However, reading complex and challenging material isn't the way the average student unwinds after a long day. Even students who love to read often find themselves overwhelmed by the amount of material they're assigned in their first year in college.

Still, reading effectively is a primary concern in just about *all* college courses, whatever the subject matter, and in nearly every college composition class you're going to have to write at least one essay that responds to a written text. In most composition classes, essays by professional writers will be central to the curriculum. Understanding what you read is crucial;

therefore, even if you initially take longer to comprehend your assignment, doing so will always pay off in time saved later on.

Timesaver Tip: Think of reading as the first step in your writing process. Because academic essays usually respond to or draw upon written work by other sources, carefully reading your assignments, and saving all the writing you do along the way, will provide you with essential material for composing your essay.

Reading Again—and Again (and Again ...)

The sooner you accept the fact that reading is a central part of your college education, the sooner you can set about devising ways to make the reading easier and more time efficient.

In the Introduction, you saw how breaking large writing assignments into smaller chunks makes them easier to complete. That's certainly the case with reading as well, with the need to prioritize being just as crucial. As you decide on a reading schedule, ask yourself the following questions:

- How long and how difficult is the reading? Is it a brief personal opinion piece or a dense article on international politics? Do I have any background knowledge of the subject matter?
- How long do I think it will realistically take to complete the reading, and when am I supposed to complete it?
- How will I be assessed on the reading? A quiz? An exam? An essay?
- How soon after the reading is due will that assessment take place?
- What are the consequences of *not* doing the reading? Looking foolish in class? Failing an important quiz? Failing the class itself?

For most college writing classes, the readings, at least initially, are fairly short. Try to read assignments of fewer than 10 pages at least twice, ideally more. If you're a slow reader, that means not waiting until the night before an assignment is due.

Rereading a short assignment the night before it is discussed has the advantage of making you look smart in class. Moreover, college professors love to give reading quizzes, and these quizzes often focus on specifics that you will have forgotten if the text is no longer fresh in your memory.

Before diving into an assigned reading, it's usually a good idea to **preview**, or look over, the text. Here are some useful questions to ask when previewing a piece of writing:

- What is the tone of the title? Funny? Serious? Threatening? Pleading?
- As you skim through the article, what jumps out at you? Are there any visuals? Words in bold or colored fonts?
- Jot down the titles of any headings in the piece. What purpose do they appear to serve?
- Reread the introduction and conclusion. What seems to be the author's main point?
- What, if anything, does the author want you do to do after reading the piece?
- Where was the piece published? Is it difficult for a writer to be published in that venue, or can anyone post anything?

Pre-reading strategies are important, but you'll need to follow a preview with a **close reading**, which means paying careful and sustained attention to the text in front of you. I'll talk about strategies for close reading throughout the rest of this chapter, but one important point to remember is that it will require you to *slow down*. You skim something because you want to get through it quickly and identify the main points. You read something carefully because someone—usually your instructor—has told you it's worth getting to know better. It's like the difference between chatting briefly with someone online and going out on an actual date. There's a commitment involved in close reading, even if, as in the case of a very short essay, it's only a commitment of fifteen or twenty minutes.

Of course, if you're assigned a book-length work of nonfiction or fiction, you'll need more concentration and more *time*, which returns us to our earlier discussion of the need to prioritize, to guard those rare empty slots in your schedule, and to say no to passing temptations. Entering a difficult text is like entering the virtual world of a video game whose rules you don't immediately understand. You need to hang around for a while and figure things out. The more challenging the material, the more frequently you'll need to return to it, and the more slowly you'll have to proceed.

Timesaver Tip: Assess the importance of each reading. You can often tell how important a reading is from the syllabus and your instructor's in-class comments. Give each reading assignment its proper due: don't make the mistake of spending tons of time on a piece that is obviously of limited importance, while skimming over something that is crucial to the class.

Reading in a Productive Space

In the previous chapter, I talked about the benefits of writing in a quiet place. The same goes for reading, only more so. When you're writing, your brain is actively constructing meaning. It has to function whether it wants to or not, so it can often muscle its way through distractions. When you read, though, it's easier to lose focus and let your mind drift from the text.

Students know that finding a quiet place isn't as easy as teachers think. As noted in the introduction, minimizing distractions is key. If you can't escape the din of a noisy living environment, there are always earplugs. Or maybe you prefer to muffle the chaos with ear buds and some soothing instrumental music. And don't forget proper lighting: you shouldn't have to strain to see the words.

In the past, someone may have told you that the only way to study was to cram for hours, but we retain material best when our minds are fresh. If you reach a point where you're no longer assimilating the assigned material, it's best to take a break, to stretch or get some exercise.

Finally, when you reach a wall and feel as though you never want to look at another clump of letters for the rest of your life, remember that no matter what you're reading—even if the subject is far from your normal areas of interest—you're learning new information about the world, or new ways of thinking about yourself. Isn't that one of the reasons you came to college in the first place?

A Sample Article

We've been discussing reading strategies without having an actual reading to examine, so let's look at the sort of short piece that might be assigned early in a writing class. The following editorial appeared as a "My Turn" column in *Newsweek* magazine in September of 2000. The author is Audrey Rock-Richardson and the title is "Pay Your Own Way (Then Thank Mom)." Most of the articles you read for this class will make fuller use of secondary sources—that is, supporting evidence by other authors—and I'll discuss the use of secondary sources extensively later in the book. However, for now, let's focus on the argument Rock-Richardson makes and how she uses personal experience to justify her beliefs. (Note: the paragraphs below are numbered so that we can refer back to them more easily.)

Pay Your Own Way (Then Thank Mom)
Audrey Rock-Richardson

[1] Is it me, or are students these days lazy? I'm not talking about tweens who don't want to do their homework or make their bed. I'm referring to people in legal adulthood who are in the process of making hugely consequential life decisions. And collectively, their attitude is that they simply cannot pay for college.

[2] Don't get me wrong. I realize that there are people out there who pay their own tuition. I know that some cannot put themselves through school because of disabilities or extenuating circumstances. But I have to say: the notion that parents must finance their children's education is ridiculous.

[3] During college I consistently endured comments from peers with scholarships and loans, peers who had new Jeeps and expensive apartments, all who would say to me, eyes bulging, "You mean your parents didn't help you at all?"

[4] I resented my fellow students for asking this, first because they made it sound like my parents were demons, and second because they were insinuating that I wasn't capable of paying my own way. "How did you pay tuition?" they'd ask. My response was simple: "I worked." They would look at me blankly, as though I had told them I'd gone to the moon.

[5] As an undergrad (University of Utah, 1998), I put myself through two solid years of full-tuition college by working as a day-care provider for $4.75 an hour. I then married and finished out seven more quarters by working as an interpreter for the deaf and a tutor in a private school.

[6] I didn't work during high school or save for years. I simply got a job the summer following graduation and worked 40 hours a week. I didn't eat out every weekend, shop a lot or own a car. I sacrificed. I was striving for something bigger and longer-lasting than the next kegger.

[7] Looking at the numbers now, I'm not sure how I managed to cover all the costs of my education. But I did. And I bought every single textbook and pencil myself, too.

[8] I remember sitting in a classroom one afternoon during my senior year, listening to everyone introduce themselves. Many students mentioned their part-time jobs. There were several members of a sorority in the class. When it came to the first girl, she told us her name and that she was a sophomore. "Oh," she added, "I major in communications." After an awkward silence, the teacher asked, "Do you work?"

[9] "Oh, no," she said emphatically, "I go to school full time." (As if those of us who were employed weren't really serious about our classes.)

[10] The girl went on to explain that her parents were paying tuition and for her to live in a sorority house (complete with a cook, I later found out). She was taking roughly 13 credit hours. And she was too busy to work.

[11] I, on the other hand, was taking 18, count 'em, 18 credit hours so I could graduate within four years. I worked 25 hours a week so my husband and I could pay tuition without future loan debt. And here's the kicker: I pulled straight A's.

[12] I caught a glimpse of that same girl's report card at the end of the quarter, and she pulled C's and a few B's, which didn't surprise me. Having to juggle tasks forces you to prioritize, a skill she hadn't learned.

[13] I'm weary of hearing kids talk about getting financial help from their parents as though they're entitled to it. I am equally tired of hearing stressed-out parents groaning, "How are we going to pay for his or her college?" Why do they feel obligated?

[14] I do not feel responsible for my daughter's education. She'll find a way to put herself through if she wants to go badly enough. And (I'm risking sounding like my mom here), she'll thank me later. I can say this because I honestly, wholeheartedly thank my parents for giving me that experience.

[15] I'm not saying that it's fun. It's not. I spent the first two years of school cleaning up after 4-year-olds for the aforementioned $4.75 an hour and taking a public bus to campus. My husband and I spent the second two struggling to pay our tuition. We lived in a cinder-block apartment with little privacy and no dishwasher.

[16] Lest I sound like a hypocrite, yes, I would have taken free college money had the opportunity presented itself. However, because my parents put themselves through school they expected me to do the same. And, frankly, I'm proud of myself. I feel a sense of accomplishment that I believe I couldn't have gained from 50 college degrees all paid for by someone else.

[17] Getting through school on our own paid off in every way. My husband runs his own business, a demanding but profitable job. I write part time and work as a mother full time. I believe the fact that we are happy and financially stable is a direct result of our learning how to manage time and money in college.

[18] So, kids, give your parents a break. Contrary to popular belief, you can pay tuition by yourself. And you might just thank your mother for it, too.

ANNOTATION

Earlier, we discussed the importance of slowing down when closely reading a text. One of the best ways to slow down is to **annotate**, that is, to make notes or comments on your reading. Annotation requires you to stay focused and actively engage with the text. Even in the digital age, the easiest way to annotate remains taking a pen or pencil to a printed page. When you do so:

- Try to identify the thesis, or main point.
- Write short questions in the margins.
- Circle words you need to look up.
- Note passages where you disagree with the author.
- Note places where the same idea occurs more than once.
- Use arrows to connect important passages.
- Highlight or underline material that you think is significant. Note: make sure you're selectively marking material. A paragraph covered in fluorescent yellow has as little value as one with no highlighting at all.

There's nothing like practice, so before you look at the annotation in Figure 2.1, go back and try annotating the first three paragraphs of "Pay Your Own Way." When you're finished, compare what you've done with what's in the book. What does the textbook point out that you wish you'd noticed? What did you see that I missed? (While you can obviously skip ahead and read my annotation, why not try it yourself first to see how you do?)

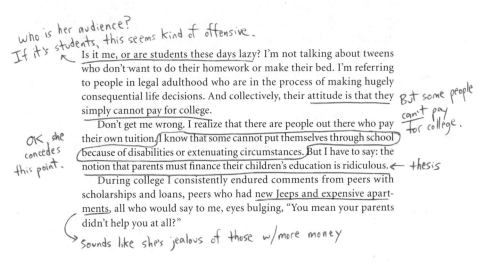

Figure 2.1 *Annotation of First Three Paragraphs*

As an active reader, what you think about the text is as important as what the author has written. Active reading is **critical reading**, which means refusing to take *anything* for granted. One benefit of critical reading is that even when your assignment is on the dull side, your engagement with it doesn't have to be. Your pen or pencil should be flying as you engage with the author as though the two of you were sitting in a coffee house having an animated conversation.

Another mark of a strong reader is the unwillingness to tolerate confusion. If you don't know what something means, you make every effort to find out. You can't do that if you're a "hands-off" reader. If you don't understand a piece, your commentary on it will be inaccurate, hazy, and just plain boring.

If your vocabulary isn't as strong as you might wish, be sure to look up any word that you can't confidently define. Back in the day, that meant keeping a dictionary nearby, but now you're just an app on your phone or an icon on your desktop away from a definition. Of course, writing down or typing the definition will help you retain it, and as you build your vocabulary, your reading speed and comprehension will increase.

One sure-fire way to identify the words you don't know in a difficult reading is to circle them as you go along. Don't worry about defining the words on your first reading—just do the best you can to make sense of the piece. Then look up each word, write down its definition, and take another shot at the reading: you'll be surprised how much clearer it is the second time around.

Some students refrain from writing in their books because they plan on selling the book back to the bookstore after the class is over, but that's short-sighted. The bookstore at my college estimates that the difference between returning a textbook that's used and unmarked versus one that's used and heavily annotated is about five dollars. In other words, your understanding of the material, and therefore your grade in this class, can be significantly improved for the price of a decent cheeseburger.

DOUBLE-ENTRY JOURNAL

Annotations, while necessary, can be messy. If you'd like to write out more substantial commentary that you might use later in your own essay, consider creating a **double-entry journal**. Making a double-entry journal is easy. Draw a line down the middle of a piece of paper. On the left side write "Summary," and on the right side put "Response." Now jot down each of the essay's main points on the left; this is basically the "What *It* Said" side. Then respond with comments and questions in the right-hand column, the "What *I* Think About It" side. Take a look at Figure 2.2, which contains responses to several points made by Audrey Rock-Richardson:

Summary	Response
—Rock-Richardson thinks it's "ridiculous" for parents to have to pay for their kids' education.	—Frankly, I think her thesis says more about her than it does about other students. Okay, her parents refused to pay for her college and she figured out how to get a degree. That's great. But why should every other student be subject to the same conditions? Lots of parents have great memories of their college days, and they want their children to have the same sense of freedom and fun. What's wrong with that?
—Toward the end of the essay, Rock-Richardson admits that she "would have taken free college money had the opportunity presented itself."	—This point seems to undercut a lot of her self-righteousness. She goes on to say that she's "proud" she didn't ever have the opportunity to get that extra money, but isn't that sour grapes, like saying, "I'm so glad I ran out of gas and had to push my car for a mile—it was really great exercise!"

Figure 2.2   *Double-Entry Journal*

ANALYSIS

Rhetorical Analysis

What we've just being doing—closely reading, commenting on, agreeing or arguing with the text—might be called **rhetorical analysis**: looking at how an author, her text, and her audience interact with one another.

"Rhetoric" is a loaded word these days, but it doesn't have to equal "insincerity." In the past, mastering rhetoric—the art of persuasive speaking and writing—was considered a cornerstone of education, so much so that books like this one, which describe ways for students to become better writers, are often called "rhetorics." Think about it: we still know the names of famous rhetoricians like Plato and Aristotle and Cicero, even if we haven't read their work.

And rhetorical analysis is not as scary as it sounds. Some instructors might argue it's just a fancy way of saying "close reading."

Here is a list of questions you might think of as follow-ups to the preview questions. If you want to know *why* you find a writer's work persuasive or unconvincing, the answer may lie in your responses:

- Who is the author?
- What is the author's thesis and overall argument?
- What assumptions is the author making?
- What evidence does the author offer to support his or her claim?
- Who is the primary audience for the piece?
- Who is the secondary audience?
- Is the author knowledgeable and even-handed in her discussion?

"Genre" is a big word in composition these days. A **genre** is a category of writing. It could mean anything from a poem or a play to a blog post or an advertisement. The main thing to remember is that each genre of writing employs its own widely acknowledged set of forms and techniques. *Where* a piece of writing appears is important because different audiences have different expectations.

We don't, for instance, expect the same formality in a Facebook post that we'd want to see in an editorial written for the *New York Times*. Before they were phased out, the "My Turn" columns in *Newsweek* were generally informal, like Rock-Richardson's, but readers could assume the assertions in the essay had been fact-checked by the magazine's editors.

Still, as active, critical readers, we may well ask questions of Rock-Richardson. Why was it so important for her to argue in a national magazine that students ought to pay for their own college education? Does she honestly believe working and going to school leads to happiness and personal responsibility, or is she just jealous of all the students who got a free ride? Is she exaggerating how much she worked and how little money she made? Did she really think she could change her readers' minds? Did she change yours?

Analyzing Visuals

We'll be looking more closely at how you might use images in your own writing in Chapters 7 and 10. For now, let's think about how visuals can be analyzed in conjunction with their accompanying text. If you're assigned a reading that includes photos or drawings or charts and graphs, you'll want to ask yourself how they support, contradict, or complicate the written text.

"Pay Your Own Way" contains no visuals, but suppose the article had included two photographs: one of several college-aged girls getting sloppy drunk, and another of a diligent-looking young woman at a job with cash in her hand. If we have been influenced by North America's culture of hard work, we would probably look down our noses at the women in the first photograph while admiring the woman in the second.

And the power of these visuals would be conveyed by *implication*: we readers would infer that the drunk girls were meant to represent the sorority girls in Rock-Richardson's class, who presumably were always at "the next kegger," while the hardworking girl was a stand-in for the author herself. We might come to these conclusions even if we assumed that the images had no personal connection to the author or her essay whatsoever.

That's something of a trick, obviously, and genre really matters here. We're generally skeptical of the images used in advertising. We know that just because we use a certain toothpaste or deodorant, we're not really going to be overwhelmed with admirers. However, we may be less on our guard when an image appears in an established magazine, or a textbook.

Let's take a brief detour from "Pay Your Own Way" and look at this photograph from 1912 to see how a single relatively neutral image might be used by a writer. The photo was taken by Lewis Wickes Hines and has the somewhat bland title of "Workers at the Weaving Machine." The photograph shows an early industrial factory, with three workers in the foreground attending to cotton looms. The workers appear to be well-dressed, but because their backs are to us, we cannot see the expressions on their faces.

Workers at the Weaving Machine

Suppose the photo appeared in an article entitled "Workers Earn a Living Wage for the First Time, Thanks to the Weaving Machine." You might think, "How lucky these three people are to have safe, steady jobs. They must be relatively happy in their work."

Then imagine how quickly your opinion of this image would change if the photograph appeared in an article about the horrors of the Industrial Age called "Workers Exploited at a Weaving Machine." Suddenly, these "faceless" laborers have become victims of capitalism rather than beneficiaries of new technology.

The picture, of course, hasn't changed at all, but the context in which it appears has forced you to interpret it in vastly different ways. It *seems* like solid evidence, but, really, what exactly does it prove?

SUMMARY

Up to this point, we've been responding to Rock-Richardson's article primarily to tease out and respond to its main points. However, the ultimate of aim of reading in a college class is usually to respond in some way to the article.

Let's say the assignment for your first essay is to state the extent to which you agree or disagree with "Pay Your Own Way (Then Thank Mom)." Essays responding to a single article typically begin by summarizing that article. Your reader needs to quickly distinguish what the other person is saying from what you're saying, and a clear, concise summary allows you to acknowledge the important points of the text you're writing about and then move on to your own ideas.

Identifying an article writer's ideas so that you can differentiate them from your own may sound like a straightforward process, but it turns out to be more problematic than you might think, which is why so many college professors consider summary such a crucial part of academic writing.

As a reminder, a **summary** is a concise statement of the main points found in a piece of writing. As you attempt to summarize a reading, keep in mind the following tips:

- A short summary uses only your own words.
- Longer summaries may very briefly borrow the writer's language, but if you do, you need to quote those words or phrases.
- A summary should be accurate and objective: this is not the place to begin arguing your own point of view.
- A summary should indicate the source, including the author and the title of her or his piece.

Without gazing down the page, see if you can summarize this article. Remember to leave out the details and use your own words. And be sure you tell us the author and the title of the work.

_____

_____

_____

_____

_____

Here's my attempt:

In her essay, "Pay Your Own Way (Then Thank Mom)," Audrey Rock-Richardson argues that covering their own college education expenses teaches students the value of responsibility and hard work, making them more likely to be happy and self-sufficient after graduation.

It's not perfect, but this summary manages to tick off the points listed on the previous page. It uses only my own words; it's accurate and objective; and it indicates the source, including the author and the title of the piece.

Summarizing this article turns out to be relatively painless because much of the piece is taken up with Rock-Richardson's specific examples of how hard she worked in comparison to her fellow students. Those are the very details that *shouldn't* be part of a summary; leaving them out makes it easier to isolate her main points.

Unless your instructor indicates otherwise, summaries don't have to be a single sentence. Also, you'll notice that in the previous paragraph I refer to the author as "Rock-Richardson" rather than "Audrey." The conventions of academic writing require us to use the author's last name.

Summarizing requires you to look closely at the material, to differentiate between a main point and a supporting detail. If you can accurately summarize a complex reading, then you've understood it. It's a skill you'll use in every class you take, and, most likely, throughout your working life.

REVERSE OUTLINE

If you're having trouble summarizing a reading, you might try a "reverse outline." Usually when you make an outline, you're doing it in preparation for writing an essay. In a **reverse outline**, by contrast, you already have the essay, so you fill in the outline by identifying the thesis, topic sentences, and main pieces of evidence. (See Chapter 4 for a full discussion of thesis and organization.) If the margins are large enough, you can write the reverse outline on the page itself, although this exercise generally looks neater and is easier to follow if you use your own paper and start from scratch.

A reverse outline of "Pay Your Own Way" might look like this:

Para.1: Hook: Students these days are lazy.

Para. 2: Thesis: Parents shouldn't have to finance their children's educations.

Para. 3–4: Examples of how other students responded when learning the author paid for her own education.

Para. 5–6: Specifics of how much the author worked to pay for school.

Para. 7: The author takes a moment to brag about her achievement.

Para. 8–12: Comparison between the author and a sorority girl who had much more free time but still received lower grades.

Para. 13–14: A reiteration of how much the author dislikes hearing how parents ought to finance their children's college education, with an acknowledgment that she does not intend to pay for her own daughter's college education.

Para. 15–17: A refutation of potential counterarguments, with the author conceding that putting herself though school was hard and admitting she would have accepted "free college money" if it had been offered; however, she is proud that she finished college on her own, and believes that it has made her financially stable.

Para. 18: Conclusion: Kids might just thank their parents for making them pay their own tuition.

The benefit of reverse outlining is that it forces you to understand the article. You can't summarize another writer's main points unless you can identify them. What you end up with is a handy synopsis of your assigned reading—a sure way to save time when you need to go back and respond to the article in an essay.

PARAPHRASE

Another common way of digesting an author's ideas is through paraphrase. To **paraphrase** is to rephrase something said or written by someone else in your own words. While you *can* use the writer's own language in a paraphrase, you'll only want to use a word or short phrase, and you'll need to put it in quotation marks.

Let's try it with the second paragraph, which reads:

> Don't get me wrong. I realize that there are people out there who pay their own tuition. I know that some cannot put themselves through school because of disabilities or extenuating circumstances. But I have to say: the notion that parents must finance their children's education is ridiculous.

Again, this isn't a test; it's an opportunity to practice a skill—try to refrain from looking ahead. Use your own words, and assume this is the first time your reader is hearing the paraphrase, so identify the author and the title of her essay:

_____

_____

_____

_____

_____

An early version of a paraphrase might look something like this:

> In her essay, "Pay Your Own Way (Then Thank Mom)," Audrey Rock-Richardson admits there are people out there who cover their own tuition. She also realizes certain students cannot put themselves through college because of disabilities or extenuating circumstances. Overall, Rock-Richardson thinks the idea of parents having to pay for their kids' education is ridiculous.

However, that's a little too close to the original, in terms of both sentence structure and word choice. If the passage appeared in your essay, technically your instructor could cite you for **plagiarism**, passing off someone else's work as your own, even though you weren't trying to steal the material.

We'll discuss plagiarism more in Chapter 9 and in Appendix II, but it's worth noting here that credit must be given for every direct quotation. Even though this version acknowledges its source, the lack of quotation marks means the writer "borrowed" that material from someone else without giving him or her due credit. The underlined passages show where this paraphrase inadvertently uses Rock-Richardson's own language:

In her essay, "Pay Your Own Way (Then Thank Mom)," Audrey Rock-Richardson admits <u>there are people out there who</u> cover <u>their own tuition</u>. She also realizes certain students <u>cannot put themselves through</u> college <u>because of disabilities or extenuating circumstances</u>. Overall, Rock-Richardson thinks the idea of parents having to pay for their kids' <u>education is ridiculous</u>.

Let's try again:

In her essay, "Pay Your Own Way (Then Thank Mom)," Audrey Rock-Richardson acknowledges not everyone can cover the expenses of higher education. She is sympathetic to disabled students and those with "extenuating circumstances." However, she completely rejects the idea that parents should be responsible for funding their children's time in college.

This is much better, accurately representing Rock-Richardson's ideas in words that are almost entirely our own.

As you transition from reading to writing, and back again, you'll find that paraphrasing has several other advantages. It allows you to refer directly to the work you're discussing without over-quoting the author. Moreover, if the reading you're referring to contains material that is valuable to your argument but is poorly or carelessly worded, a paraphrase allows you to acknowledge your source while giving the author's words some much-needed polishing.

QUOTATIONS

Strong quotations can be the highlight of an academic essay, and we'll talk extensively about quoting, one of the three important methods of extracting material from a reading, in Chapter 7. However, when you're trying to understand the gist of a reading, summary and paraphrase are generally far more useful. In fact, focusing too much on the proper formatting for a quotation can be distracting. Therefore, for now, we'll just mention a few basics.

When you quote from a source, you must:

- use the source's *exact* words;
- place quotation marks around the quotation;
- indicate the source of the quotation.

For example, a quotation from a book on first-generation college students might look like this:

In their book *First-Generation College Students: Understanding and Improving the Experience from Recruitment to Commencement,* Lee Ward, Michael J. Siegel, and Zebulun Davenport argue that "any amount of college education received by the parents of first-generation students is an important factor in how they view and experience college" (5).

The material inside the quotation marks represents what the authors actually wrote, word for word. While the **signal phrase** indicating the book's authors and title is a bit cumbersome, it's useful for readers to know right from the start the source of the quotation. (The parenthetical page number at the end is an example of MLA style documentation; it also requires an end citation in a Works Cited page, all of which we'll cover in Appendix II.)

Questions and Suggestions FOR You

1. Go back and reread "Pay Your Own Way (Then Thank Mom)." When you're finished, describe your reading process. Did you read straight through without stopping? Did you pause to look up any words? Did you find yourself gazing off at times to digest the content and compare it to your own experience? When were you most and least engaged in the essay?

2. Talking about your reading assignment after you've finished it is important. Find someone willing to listen to you for a few minutes and discuss this chapter's content. Describe the encounter. Did your listener ask any questions or make any comments that caused you to think differently about the chapter?

3. Summarize the main points of this chapter in a sentence or two. Remember to use your own words and be accurate and objective.

4. Choose a short paragraph from this chapter and paraphrase it. Use your own words whenever possible, and use quotation marks if you borrow any language.

5. Annotate one page of this chapter. Make comments or ask questions in the margins, and circle or underline significant words, phrases, or sentences. Use lines and arrows to connect important passages.

6. Read another article, perhaps one assigned by your instructor, which uses supporting evidence from outside the author's own personal experience. Annotate and summarize the article, making sure to identify which material is written by the author and which is supporting

evidence written by someone else. When do the "secondary sources" effectively buttress the author's claims? At what points are personal opinion and experience more useful in making the argument?

7. Look at your syllabus for this class and skim over your assigned readings. Which assignments look good? Not-so-good? Why?

8. How do your readings for this class compare with your readings for the other classes you are taking this term? Are the assignments for this class longer or shorter? More difficult or less? Are there any possible connections between the subject matter in your writing class and in your other classes?

9. The Questions and Suggestions in Chapter 1 asked about your history as a writer. Compose a similar response based on your history as a reader. Begin with the first time you can remember reading words on paper or a computer screen and go all the way to the present. Questions 10–13 might be incorporated into this narrative, or your instructor may ask you to answer them separately.

10. What's the most important thing you've ever read and why?

11. What are your biggest challenges as a reader? What are your strongest biases? If English is not your native language, what difficulties have you faced when reading another language?

12. What issues are most likely to interfere with your success as a reader this term? Make a list, and then brainstorm a possible solution for each potential problem.

13. List all the places where you read regularly, and identify the locations you think will be most conducive to the academic reading you'll be doing in this class.

Questions and Suggestions FROM You

List three questions you still have after reading this section. Start by reviewing the chapter. If that method doesn't inspire three questions, think about the overall topic of reading for college. What don't you know about academic reading that you would really like to know?

1. _____

_____

_____

_____

_____

2. _____

_____

_____

_____

_____

3. _____

_____

_____

_____

_____

Describe one activity related to academic reading *not mentioned in this chapter* that you think would be helpful to do in class. Again, any successful activity in any course you've ever taken might serve as a model.

_____

_____

_____

_____

_____

CHAPTER THREE

Ideas into Text

GETTING STARTED

LIGHTNING RESEARCH

INVENTION

THE THREE APPEALS

DISCUSSION

SOONER RATHER THAN LATER

GETTING STARTED

For many students, just getting started can be the most difficult writing task. As novelist Neil Gaiman says, "Being a writer is a very peculiar sort of a job: it's always you versus a blank sheet of paper (or a blank screen) and quite often the blank piece of paper wins."

Of course, while it might be comforting to know that even bestselling authors have trouble writing, that doesn't help *you* much when you have an essay to finish and a deadline to meet. Fortunately, over the years, writers have come up with a number of strategies for generating ideas and turning them into text, many of which we will discuss in this chapter.

Don't get frustrated, though, if your first tactic doesn't work. Maybe freewriting doesn't pan out this time, so you try doing additional research on your topic. Perhaps talking with your best friend about the assignment is a bust, but things start to click when you make a list of everything you know about the subject, and everything you need to know. Make a "cluster," ask the "journalist's questions," analyze your audience. *Some* strategy for getting started will eventually pay off.

If you are given complete freedom to choose your own topic, you'll want to find something you can write about with passion. Essayist Phillip Lopate advises students to "figure out something on your own, some question to which you don't already have the answer when you start." For Lopate, this often involves extending sympathy to those who are unlike us: "We know we should be more open to others, but we're very self-pre-occupied." Investigating the lives and opinions of "the other" can be a fascinating way into an essay.

In first- and second-year classes, however, instructors are more likely to provide their students with a list of focused **writing prompts**, or assignments. Let's say, for example, that your first assignment of the semester is this: "Write an essay on the challenges first-generation college students face when attempting to complete their undergraduate degrees."

Usually, your professor will provide further instructions, either in class or as part of the prompt, but suppose the sentence above is all you have to go on. What in the world do you do first?

LIGHTNING RESEARCH

Author Geoff Dyer's motto is "If you're not overprepared, you're underprepared." You'll probably do the bulk of your research *after* you've crafted a thesis and sketched out a plan for your essay, skills we'll cover in the next chapter, but in the Internet Age we tend to look first for answers online, almost without thinking.

In the early days of the Internet, professors would nearly always suggest that students begin their research with print sources. Now, of course, most professors themselves begin researching online, and this book assumes that when you're really curious about a topic, the first thing you're likely to do is run an Internet search, most likely on Google, or to see if there is a relevant Wikipedia page.

You might think of your initial searches as "lightning research." At this stage, you want credible sources, of course, but you should primarily be getting an overview of your topic, as though you were flying above a small country in an airplane, noting a mountain range here, a coastline there, a large city somewhere in between. In lightning research, a source that you wouldn't necessarily cite in an academic essay—someone responding to a blog or answering a question on Ask.com—might still bring up a point that is worth pursuing with more credible sources.

Chapter 5 is devoted to research, in particular to assessing the validity of the sources you plan to use. The focus of this chapter is on the very early stages of planning, when you're looking for relationships between ideas and generating connections that didn't immediately occur to you.

So once you sit down and make that initial search on Google or Bing or Wikipedia, what do you do with the results? Two basic strategies are particularly useful:

1. *Make notes as ideas occur to you.* There's nothing quite like that first flush of recognition: "*Ah*, that's how these two apparently unlike ideas might be linked." Unfortunately, these moments of recognition can be fleeting, so you want to write them down as they occur to you, either in a notebook or in a digital document.
2. *Store the results of your most productive searches.* That could mean bookmarking a site, or printing it out, or emailing yourself a link. It's best, obviously, to include a brief note summarizing the contents of the site.

Look over what you have, and, without yet getting too bogged down in individual sources, use what you've learned in the first twenty or thirty minutes to play around with your ideas, to group those theories and examples that seem to be related.

INVENTION

Freewriting

Classical rhetoricians used the term "invention" to describe the full range of getting-started activities. We'll look specifically at Aristotle and one of his most famous invention techniques in the next section, but let's begin with an activity for turning ideas into text that you are probably already familiar with: freewriting.

Professor Peter Elbow advises students, "Do lots of freewriting and raw writing and exploration of the topic—writing in whatever style comes out. Put all your effort into finding the best ideas and arguments you can, and don't worry about your tone." Elbow isn't alone in championing freewriting. Just about any writer who's ever been blocked has used this technique as a way to overcome that inner critic who is perpetually dissatisfied.

The "rules" of freewriting are pretty basic: Choose a short amount of time—five, ten, or fifteen minutes are standard—then start writing, and don't stop until the time is up. Don't worry about spelling or grammar or style—just see what you can come up with in a limited chunk of time.

Here's a five-minute freewrite on our essay topic about the challenges first-generation college students face:

I'm not a first-generation college student so right away I'm thinking this is not going to be an easy topic for me. On the other hand, I do know a lot of first-generation students, well, not a lot, but some. There are some in our class, I know from the first day's introduction.

In fact, the guy sitting next to me is first-generation, I'm pretty sure. I could ask him about his experiences. But how? Isn't he going to be offended if I'm using him as the subject of my experiment? But maybe I'm overthinking it. Maybe he *wants* to talk about it. Maybe I could ask the teacher after class what she thinks, or she could tell everyone, if you're willing to talk about your experiences with other students, let everyone know. That's actually a really good idea.

While there's not much, if any, material that could actually be used in an essay, this freewrite has managed to 1) recognize a potential problem with the assignment (the writer is not a first-generation college student), 2) identify a possible work-around (talking to a classmate who is), 3) detect a second potential problem (asking that student for information could be awkward), and 4) formulate a way to gather the information (asking the instructor to make a full-class announcement).

In her excellent book *Writing Down the Bones*, Natalie Goldberg argues for freewriting because of its ability to cut us loose from feeling responsible for every utterance we jot down on the page. "We think our words are permanent and solid and stamp us forever," Goldberg says. "That's not true. We write in the moment." For Goldberg and Elbow, and so many others, the beauty of freewriting is not only the freedom promised in its name, but how quickly it can be done and how frequently it generates something useful for the writer.

Listing

When you go grocery shopping for the week, chances are you make a list beforehand. If you're savvy, you try and organize the list by which items are in which aisles, but even if you just jot down what you need on a piece of paper, you're in much better shape than if you went to the store unprepared. Not having a list means you are more likely to wander aimlessly, to buy things you don't need, and to forget the things that you do.

In his article "10 Reasons Why We Love Making Lists," journalist Linton Weeks sings the praises of list-making, pointing out that lists "bring order to chaos," "help us remember things," and "relieve stress and focus the mind." Billionaire Richard Branson is another advocate of making lists. Among Branson's tips are "Always carry a notebook," "Write down every single idea you have, no matter how big or small," and "Make your goals measurable so you know if your plans are working."

You'll find that many of the virtues of lists in general apply to those you make when preparing to write your essay. Lists help you focus on your writing task, remind you of what you've been thinking, and let you know which issues you've addressed and which you haven't. Like freewriting, listing releases the writer from any obligation to show cause and effect or to favor one idea over another. Therefore, a list, like a freewrite, tends to have the same feeling of randomness. However, unlike a freewrite, a list can be as long or short as you want.

A quick list generated on the topic of the challenges faced by first-generation college students might look something like this:

- I need to do some research on first-generation college students.
- What percentage are they of the total population of incoming freshman?
- So, statistics (ask professor or tutor where to look).
- My professor keeps saying a general Web search is mostly a waste of time. So Google Scholar or Google Books? Library database?
- It would also be good to get the *stories* of first-generation students. What did they face before college? How hard was it to get here?
- Interview guy who sits next to me?
- Are there any movies on this?
- How realistic is it for these students to actually finish college? (That sounds harsher than I mean it to.) Statistics again.
- What exactly *are* the challenges? List them all, then look for the ones that seem easiest to write about.

Often, one item in a list will seem particularly promising, and that item can generate its own list. Suppose this student finds the idea of interviewing his classmate a particularly promising source of information. This might, in turn, lead to a list of interview questions:

- Where were you born?
- Where were your parents born?
- What do your parents do?
- Why didn't they go to college?
- Do they support your going to college?
- Why do you want to go to college?
- What's the biggest challenge you've faced so far?
- What's the biggest challenge you think you'll face in the future?

People who habitually make lists (and I confess I'm one of them) find that list-making not only brings clarity to their days, but it also helps them prioritize—to distinguish the important from the trivial. Especially if you are *not* a particularly organized person, a list can be a very useful tool, indeed. And there's nothing quite as satisfying as drawing a great big line through something you've worked hard on and finally completed.

> **Timesaver Tip: Make lists *throughout* the essay writing process**. Lists are handy for getting started on your essay, but they are also useful when you're halfway through the paper, and even when you think you're just about finished. Like a shopper making her way through a store, you can cross things off your list as you complete them so you're always sure what still needs doing and what's already been done.

Clustering

Different writers have different learning styles, and some of us need a visual element in the invention activity. Sophisticated "mind mapping" apps like iThoughtsHD can now be downloaded online, but you can still cluster the old fashioned way, with a pen and a piece of paper.

Clustering, like the other invention activities we have covered, is usually done quickly and spontaneously. Generally, a cluster begins from a

Figure 3.1   *Clustering*

single word or phrase located in the center of the page. You draw a circle or box around it, then draw a line out to the first idea you associate with the main idea. Other lines extending from the secondary idea lead to specific examples, or further sub-headings.

The point of this invention activity is to group related ideas together. Eventually, you're likely to end up with a rough outline for your essay that sometimes looks a bit like a flow chart.

Continuing with our essay about the problems first-generation college students face to complete their degrees, we might sketch out a cluster that looks like Figure 3.1.

The Journalist's Questions

Asking questions is the quickest path to answers, so you should take any opportunity you have to generate a question set. In that vein, nonfiction writers have long relied on the journalist's questions: *Who? What? When? How? Where? Why?* These one-word questions help journalists thrown into the midst of a chaotic scene to remember to get the basic information for their stories. The questions turn out to be equally useful when writing a celebrity profile—or an academic essay.

As with the other invention activities, the journalist's questions have no single "correct" outcome—they are instead designed to help you find your way into your essay. Here are just a few of the many possible questions that might result from using these key questions for our essay on first-generation college students:

- *Who* are first-generation students?
- *What* do they have in common? What are their main problems, their main goals?
- *When* did they make their decision to come to college? Is this something recent, or have they been thinking about it since they were children? Do their parents support their decision to become college students?
- *How* will they cope with being first-generation students? Will they get extra support services? Will they isolate themselves from non-first-generation students?
- *Where* are they coming from? Are they mostly locals, or from other states, provinces, or countries?
- *Why* are they the first in their families to go to college? Was it difficult to make the leap to college? What prevented their parents from attending college? Why are they at our particular campus?

As you can see, one question quickly leads to another, with the activity generating multiple avenues for further research.

Journaling

One of the most time-honored ways for writers to generate raw material they may use later is to keep a journal. Granted, some students associate keeping a journal with New Age philosophies, and many of the titles of books on journaling support that belief: *Writing as a Way of Healing*, or *Creating a Visual Autobiography of Your Authentic Self*, or *A Spiritual Quest*. If you wish to find out more about your own psychological workings, a journal can be an immensely important tool. However, even if you are the sort of person who cringes when hearing terms like "Human Potential Movement" and the "Eternal Now," a journal can still be a handy repository for ideas. Think of it as a jar in which you toss loose change, knowing those coins will come in handy the next time you are broke.

Hardcore journal-keepers often decorate their journals. They draw or paint on the covers, embellish the pages, and dutifully save each journal once it is full. For others, a journal is a record of a specific time and place: throwing it away when it is complete is a sign of moving on. There was even a popular book called *Wreck This Journal* that asked its owners to chew on and poke holes in the pages, to scratch and staple them together, to cover them with mud.

Whatever you decide to do with your journal physically, turn to it mentally whenever you feel the need to record something potentially valuable. Among the most common uses for academic journals are the following:

- Responding to a reading.
- Evaluating an argument by another writer.
- Copying out quotations from other writers.
- Jotting down your own ideas.
- Asking questions.
- Providing answers.

Indeed, a writer's journal can be a home for all the invention activities we've discussed so far. As writing theorist Ken Macrorie says, "A journal is a place for confusion and certainty, for the half-formed and the completed."

Some instructors award course credit for journals which they periodically collect and evaluate. If that's the case in your class, your professor will obviously provide you with the details of what's expected of your journal. However, whether or not anyone else reads your journal, keeping one has a very significant benefit for you as a college student: it forces you to write, and the more you write, the easier writing becomes.

Timesaver Tip: Save everything you write. Whether it's a list or a cluster, a freewrite or a question set, *don't throw it away.* If you're writing on a computer, simply save the file with an easy to remember name like "Pre-writing for First-Generation Essay." Or buy a journal and become one of the many writers who have found these personal notebooks, to quote author Ralph Fletcher, the key to "unlocking the writer within you."

THE THREE APPEALS

The title of a famous scholarly article by linguist Walter J. Ong, "The Writer's Audience Is Always a Fiction," suggests a potential problem for all writers. Even when you are writing for just your professor, you will always necessarily be *imagining* your audience, who will probably be some version of yourself.

Nevertheless, most college writing instructors will expect you to have an audience in mind, even if it is partially fabricated. Therefore, let's take the prompt we've been working on and add an audience to focus the rhetorical situation:

> Write an essay on the challenges first-generation college students face when attempting to complete their undergraduate degrees. The audience for your essay is the administrators of your college. Your essay should convince them to either increase or decrease financial aid for first-generation students. Assume that funding is limited, so that if financial aid increases for these students, it will decrease for all other students, and vice versa.

Suddenly, with the addition of a few sentences, the possibilities for your essay have narrowed tremendously. Now that you know your audience, you can begin to analyze which approaches will work best to convince school administrators of your point of view.

Let's say for the moment that all the prewriting you have done so far has made you sympathetic to the challenges faced by first-generation students, so you decide to support an increase in their financial aid. How are you going to persuade administrators to follow your recommendation?

At this point, it's worth joining two thousand years of writers and turning to the Greek philosopher and rhetorician Aristotle for some advice. For Aristotle, invention meant "discovering the best possible means of persuasion." He discusses a number of activities involved with "*inventio*"—defining terms, deciding whether or not the argument is right for the venue, judging the seriousness of the topic, and so on—but perhaps his most famous invention strategies are the "three modes of persuasion" or "the three appeals":

Logos: reason
Pathos: emotions, values, and beliefs
Ethos: the speaker's and reader's credibility

When you appeal to *logos*, you speak to your audience's logical side. In an ideal world, the appeal to *logos* would be the only method of persuasion necessary. However, as you know, our world is far from ideal, so writers frequently turn to *pathos* to win over their audiences. The appeal to *pathos* stirs up an audience—it doesn't just make them think, it makes them *feel*.

If your audience already agrees with you, the appeal most likely to work is *pathos*. If you or a family member has ever donated money to a charity, you may already be familiar with the appeal to *pathos*. Nonprofit groups share mailing lists, so a $50 donation to Save the Children might result in requests for money from the Children's Health Fund, UNICEF, World Vision International, and so on. These entreaties will likely include not just heartrending text about the children's plights, but also photographs of doctors in refugee camps, their stethoscopes held against the chests of visibly starving infants whose eyes are wide and pleading. These non-profits know that you are already sympathetic to the *logos* of helping those in need, but without the persuasion of *pathos* you may be unwilling to part with your money.

On the other hand, if your audience is likely to be resistant to your argument, you need to establish your credibility as a speaker who can be trusted, this time using the appeal to *ethos*. Say, for instance, that your audience is non-first-generation students who face the prospect of losing out on financial aid. You can assume that presenting yourself *and* them as trustworthy souls who want what's best for the college—*good people*, in short—will be a useful tactic in winning some support for your cause.

Obviously, the college administrators in our prompt will have their own biases, but let's work under the assumption that they are genuinely open to both sides of the argument. As a result, they may be moved by all three of the appeals, which means it's worth jotting down some initial ideas for each mode of persuasion. Again, in this preparatory stage, your writing is likely to be informal.

Logos: I need to figure out a way to show that this is a good bottom-line decision. College administrators want their students to be successful and giving students more money for college takes pressure off them. Students won't have to work as much, or appeal to family members, etc., so they can concentrate on completing their degrees. Maybe I could also find some statistics showing that first-generation students who are well-supported by their universities tend to be especially generous alumni.

Pathos: I'm going back to the guy who sits next to me in class. A good guy—funny, smart. No doubt he can be successful. Maybe if I paint a picture of what his life—or the life of someone like him—would be if he didn't go to college, it could be pretty moving. Some emotional photos or illustrations might also help make my point.

Ethos: Because I'm not a first-generation college student myself, I should have a pretty easy time proving I'm a credible speaker. While I seem to be arguing against my own best interests, I'm doing so because I think first-generation students bring an energy and enthusiasm to the campus that make all of us better students. I'll also be appealing to my reader's credibility because college administrators, like most people, want to be thought of as generous and fair-minded.

Again, it's the rare essay that will have an entirely balanced use of all three of the modes of persuasion. However, the simple act of writing out potential arguments in each category will help significantly as you move toward crafting a thesis and outlining your essay.

Finally, as you deliberate about which appeal will best suit your prompt, don't forget your other, underlying, audience: your instructor who assigned and will grade your essay. Having listened to her or him in class, what do you think your professor values? Does she emphasize logical thinking? Does he seem particularly moved by the problems of the under-served? Yes, your essay is part of an ongoing conversation on an important topic, but you also have pragmatic reasons for writing it. Like an advertising firm designing a marketing campaign, your first pitch isn't really to the customer (your essay's imaginary audience) but to the company executive (your professor) who can either green-light your proposal—or put the kibosh on it.

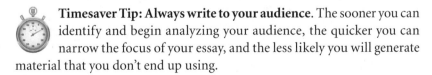 **Timesaver Tip: Always write to your audience**. The sooner you can identify and begin analyzing your audience, the quicker you can narrow the focus of your essay, and the less likely you will generate material that you don't end up using.

DISCUSSION

It's beneficial to discuss your essay throughout the writing process. You will probably want to talk about the essay prompt with your instructor or classmates before you've written a word. Then, whether you are pre-writing, drafting, or revising, you'll find that even a short verbal exchange with another person can be helpful. Indeed, one of the core principles of the National Council of Teachers of English is that "writing benefits from talking."

Here are some of the most common "discussion venues" in a writing class for generating essay ideas and some suggestions for approaching them productively.

In-Class Small Group

We'll spend more time talking about peer group discussion in the section on revision in Chapter 9. Nevertheless, while in-class small groups tend to focus on completed essay drafts, you can also get a great deal of help in the early stages of planning your essay. Classmates are able to exchange ideas in a low-risk, informal setting. You can ask questions and make comments that you might not feel comfortable trying out in front of the entire class.

If you were discussing our proposed essay on first-generation college students, for instance, you might ask how many in the group fit that description. Just hearing their stories would make for potentially strong essay material. You could also compare and contrast the challenges faced by first-generation students with those encountered by students whose parents went to college. There's a lot of valuable information to be culled from a small group, if you only take the initiative to reveal and gather it.

Finally, wherever you stand on a topic—even if you completely disagree with a classmate—listen and take notes. You never know when they may come in handy.

Full-Class

Writing professor John Ruszkiewicz acknowledges that professors, just like their counterparts in business, "admire well-prepared people who can handle themselves in public with skill and grace." One of the best ways to do this, Ruszkiewicz argues, is to let others speak first, to listen carefully to their discussion, and then to "become a connector in the group, someone who occasionally summarizes the direction of the discussion and then pushes it forward."

If you have an opinion on a topic and feel strongly enough to launch it into a full-class discussion, you are likely to receive opinions that both confirm and counter your beliefs. Go into these discussions with an open mind. It's much better to change your opinion early in the composition process and write a strong paper than to stick doggedly to a weak position just because it was the first one that occurred to you.

Again, listen and take notes. Even if the class discussion veers away from your topic, you may still get general ideas for your essay. And, of course, you can always raise your hand and steer the dialogue back toward the subject of your essay.

Informal Out-of-Class

Conversations about your essay that take place outside of class are likely to be mixed in with talk about any number of other subjects. Nevertheless, the casualness of chatting with a friend allows you to approach your topic from an unconventional, adversarial, or even comic perspective. This is a time for thinking outside the box and allowing your imagination free reign.

Unfortunately, it's easy to forget a good idea you hear in the middle of a long confab with a friend. Therefore, because good ideas are rarer than we would like them to be, it's worth pausing for a minute, taking out your notebook or your phone, and making sure that good idea isn't lost forever.

Online

With the increasing number of college classes offered online and as hybrids (part online, part face-to-face), chances are that at some point during your higher education you will be discussing classwork in a virtual environment. In an online or hybrid class, participation in discussion forums will probably be part of your class grade, so you already have an incentive to offer up your best ideas clearly and persuasively.

An even stronger incentive to participate in and monitor these virtual chats is the commentary being generated on the subject of your essay. Entering a good discussion forum is like entering a room with a lively and entertaining conversation going on: it makes you want to hang around and listen.

As you discuss issues online, you'll want to follow a few basic guidelines:

- Be prepared.
- Be polite.
- Stay on topic.
- Use concrete evidence to support your points.
- Proofread your comments at least once before posting them.

Obviously, if you borrow a specific idea from a classmate, you will want to acknowledge that fact in your essay. More frequently, though, the energy of a vigorous dialogue will inspire your own thinking to move in directions you hadn't anticipated.

Timesaver Tip: Visit your campus writing center. Most colleges and universities have writing centers, places on campus where you can meet with a tutor to talk about your writing. One of the best investments of your time—wherever you are in the writing process—is to talk over your paper with an experienced writing tutor.

Find out where your writing center is, when it's open, and whether or not you need to make an appointment in advance. Then take advantage of this invaluable resource throughout your college career.

SOONER RATHER THAN LATER

In his article "The Importance of Writing Badly," professor Bruce Ballenger remarks, "When I give my students permission to write badly, to suspend their compulsive need to find the 'perfect way of saying it,' often something miraculous happens: Words that used to trickle forth come gushing to the page." Author Allegra Goodman makes a similar point: "Writer, beware! The inner critic is insidious, subversive, always available for depressive episodes. Stay alert. Know the enemy. Know yourself."

Both Ballenger and Goodman want us to know that when we begin turning ideas into text, we need to give ourselves a break. Rather than expecting perfection from our first attempt at an assignment, we should anticipate more than a little chaos. It's a fact: the early stages of writing are often quite messy.

However, *don't give up.* You'll be surprised how helpful it is to take a short break before coming back to your writing. You didn't realize it, but while you were exercising or eating or watching TV, your brain was working on a solution to the problem.

The key, though, is giving yourself plenty of time to make mistakes, to take risks and fail. Occasionally your argument will arrive in a very coherent form, seemingly out of nowhere. More often, you'll spend a good deal of your writing time coming up with ideas and sentences and paragraphs and even entire pages that you ultimately reject.

As I've already noted, good academic writing tends to be the result of a recursive and discontinuous process. We start, we stop, we repeat, we delete. We get up, we sit down. Even when we've chained ourselves to our writing desks, writers are often thinking about something other than the text they are creating.

Ultimately, it's helpful to know your own habits as a writer. This is important because, like good reading, good writing generally takes time. Just because in the past you've always waited until the night before an essay is due to start writing, that doesn't mean it's the best way to proceed.

If you play a musical instrument, imagine how hard it would be to get up onstage and play a difficult piece with practically no rehearsal. You'd feel embarrassed to stand there fumbling your way from one note or chord to the next. Sure, if your audience was sympathetic, like many high-school teachers are—at least you showed up and gave it a try!—you might "pass" your audition. But college instructors tend to be less sympathetic to the simple act of making an effort: they want to see you actually *succeed*.

Consequently, it's best to begin the early stages of writing as soon as you receive your assignment. Put those first thoughts down on paper or in a digital document *now*. Getting to know your topic from a number of different perspectives, even if you only end up pursuing one, will make you a more authoritative and confident writer.

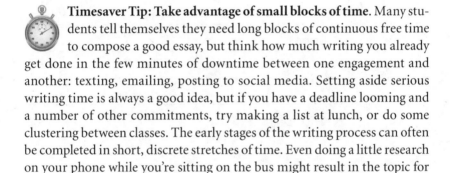

Timesaver Tip: Take advantage of small blocks of time. Many students tell themselves they need long blocks of continuous free time to compose a good essay, but think how much writing you already get done in the few minutes of downtime between one engagement and another: texting, emailing, posting to social media. Setting aside serious writing time is always a good idea, but if you have a deadline looming and a number of other commitments, try making a list at lunch, or do some clustering between classes. The early stages of the writing process can often be completed in short, discrete stretches of time. Even doing a little research on your phone while you're sitting on the bus might result in the topic for one of your paragraphs.

Questions and Suggestions FOR You

1. If you have the prompt for your first essay assignment, choose one of the invention activities above and see what you come up with.
2. Choose a second, very different, activity for turning ideas into text and see if that's more, or less, useful than the first activity.
3. Sketch out Aristotle's "three appeals" as they apply to your assignment. How can you appeal to your readers' sense of *logos*, or reason; *pathos*, or emotion; and *ethos*, or author/reader credibility?
4. Start a journal, whether it's a leather-bound volume, or a spiral notebook, or simply a file on your computer. Feel free to jot down random ideas, but keep turning your focus back to your essay assignment.

When you've filled the journal with 5 or 10 or 20 pages, underline or highlight or use a different color font to emphasize those ideas that are most likely to help with the composition of your essay.

5. Talk to someone smart and friendly about your essay topic. Record your conversation on your phone, or jot down ideas as they arise.

6. Using a daily planner, or a calendar, or just a blank piece of paper, sketch out a timeline for completing your essay. Be realistic. Allow for assignments in other classes as well as work, family obligations, and at least a bit of fun.

Questions and Suggestions FROM You

List three questions you still have after reading this section. Start by reviewing the chapter. If that method doesn't inspire three questions, think about the overall topic of turning your ideas into sentences. What don't you know about turning ideas into text that you would still like to know?

1. _____

_____

_____

_____

2. _____

_____

_____

_____

3. _____

_____

_____

_____

_____

Describe one activity related to turning ideas into text *not mentioned in this chapter* that you think would be helpful to do in class. Any successful activity in any course you've ever taken might serve as a model.

_____

_____

_____

_____

_____

CHAPTER FOUR

Arguments and Organization

THESIS STATEMENTS
OUTLINES
CONSIDERING OTHER PERSPECTIVES
TOPIC SENTENCES

THESIS STATEMENTS

I noted in the introduction that "rhetoric" these days often has a negative connotation. In everyday use, it usually means wordiness or "hot air." Similarly, the word "argument" probably evokes a couple having a shouting match on a reality TV show rather than the definition of the word as it is used in this book: "a reason or set of reasons for persuading others that an idea or action is right or wrong."

At the core of every strong academic essay is a compelling argument, and at the core of every compelling academic argument is a solid thesis: a succinct statement of the argument the writer is trying to persuade the reader to believe.

Of course, the word "thesis" can sound formal and forbidding. Many a student has cringed at the thought of having to write one. However, a thesis statement is really just a well-written summary of what you're trying to persuade your reader to believe. Think of a thesis as a handy reference point, not just for readers, but for you, the writer, as you begin the work of composing your essay.

Statement of Fact vs. Thesis Statement

As you set out to write a **working thesis**—a provisional thesis that you're willing to modify as you go—it's crucial to remember that a thesis is an argument, not a statement of fact. You can see the difference between the two in this very simple example:

Statement of Fact: The sky is blue today.

vs.

Thesis Statement: Blue is the best color for the sky.

Assuming for the moment that the sky is, indeed, blue today, there is nothing for the reader to contest. (Moreover, you can imagine how incredibly dull a paper generated by this statement of fact would be.)

Granted, our thesis statement isn't exactly scintillating, but it *could* result in something resembling an academic essay. "*Why* is blue the best color for the sky?" a reader might wonder, and the writer might respond, "Because I am a photographer and a clear sky provides the best light for taking pictures." Let's suppose, however, that the reader is also a photographer, but one who prefers shadows and grays. "No," she replies, "*gray* is the best color for the sky, not blue. When the weather is overcast, photographs have much more resonance and depth."

The moment we have a disagreement like this, each side will need to begin marshaling evidence and thinking of clever ways to present it. A thesis *generates* an academic essay in a way that a statement of fact cannot.

Topic + Comment = Thesis Statement

Typically, an academic thesis statement both announces the subject matter and makes a comment on it. In our super-basic thesis statement, the topic is the color of the sky, while the comment is that blue is the best color for the sky:

Topic (Color of the Sky) + Comment (Blue Is the Sky's Best Color) = Thesis (Blue is the best color for the sky.)

There isn't a single best way to phrase a thesis statement, but readers should be able to identify quickly what's being written about and the author's opinion of the subject matter.

Narrowing Your Topic

As we've suggested, strong thesis statements are not only arguable but also worth arguing; they must justify fuller discussion of a topic. An entire essay about the color of the sky, unless it is very creative and well written, will probably bore 99.9 per cent of readers, so let's shift to something more lively, and more likely to appear in a college class.

You'll often hear college professors talking about "narrowing your topic." The best way to narrow a topic is to think of the problem as what's referred to as a "stacked Venn diagram," with the broader topic encircling increasingly smaller sub-topics, as shown in Figure 4.1.

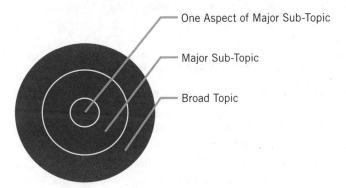

Figure 4.1   *Narrowing Your Topic*

For example, suppose you are given free rein to write about an important social issue. Maybe you've long been interested in questions surrounding what's sometimes called "the drug problem." That's certainly a narrower topic than "important social issues," but it's still too big overall. A walk around your college dorm on a Friday night might convince you that the aspect of the drug problem closest to you is the consumption of marijuana and whether or not it should be legalized.

A stacked Venn diagram showing this narrowing of your topic would look something like Figure 4.2.

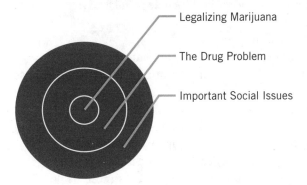

Figure 4.2   *Narrowing the "Drug Problem" Topic*

You can also graph this movement using arrows, from broad to less broad to potential essay topic:

Important Social Issues ➔ The Drug Problem ➔ Legalizing Marijuana

The legalization of marijuana is still too large a topic for a short academic essay, but now, at least, you can begin to ask productive questions about the topic as you continue to narrow it.

A Thesis Statement Answers a Question

A strong thesis statement is nearly always the answer to a question, whether that question is stated—in your instructor's prompt, for instance—or implied by the subject itself. For example, our topic suggests that prohibition of marijuana use creates as many, or more, problems than it solves. The question that arises is "Should marijuana be legalized?"

Assume that your answer is yes. Immediately, a potential reader would want to know "*Why* should we legalize marijuana?"

You may already have some answers floating around in your head. If so, the invention activities described in the previous chapter will help you turn those ideas into words. You might also do some preliminary searching on the Internet, or begin thinking about how Aristotle's "three appeals" might work on an audience, or you might just have a conversation with your instructor or a tutor or a friend.

An initial investigation into the topic could easily generate a list that looks similar to the one below.

Legalizing marijuana will:
- increase quality control;
- allow a greater number of seriously ill people to take advantage of its medicinal properties;
- decrease the money made by criminals;
- eliminate the need for expensive law enforcement;
- eliminate the need for building and maintaining prisons to house those convicted of possession;
- increase the tax base;
- eliminate the racial bias by police (non-whites are currently arrested in disproportionately high numbers for marijuana possession);
- create jobs for those who grow, sell, and regulate the drug;
- transition people away from alcohol, which poses more health risks than marijuana.

Initially, you might find the reporter in you asking a barrage of "journalist's questions": Who should be allowed to consume marijuana? What are the mechanisms necessary to put legalization into action? When should this process go into effect? How should the government collect its share of tax revenue? Where, exactly, would the marijuana be grown?

It's easy to imagine the answers to this set of questions leading to further questions, and on and on, until you might be ready to shrug your shoulders and give up. When you're digging deep into a topic, it's not hard to feel overwhelmed, so it's worth stepping back, taking a breath, and looking at your list again.

As you review these nine points, you can begin to see how some of them might naturally go together. Suppose you want to emphasize the health benefits of marijuana. You could talk about both its medical value—treatment for cancer, glaucoma, and so on—as well as the many claims that it's less harmful to most people's health than alcohol. Maybe you'd prefer to focus on social justice, the way that drug laws tend to harm the poor and people of color. Or you might feel like concentrating on financial issues. Prosecuting the War on Drugs costs a lot of money; moreover, if marijuana were legal, the tax revenue generated by legitimate sales would surely be substantial.

Let's say that last cluster of ideas, on economic concerns, seems the most promising to you. You ask the question once more, and then provide a clear and specific answer that will serve as your working thesis:

Q. Why should we legalize marijuana?
A. Legalizing marijuana will improve our economy. Legalization will eliminate the need for costly enforcement of marijuana laws. It will also reduce the expense of building and maintaining prisons because fewer people will be incarcerated. Our government not only will save money, but will also collect revenue through sales tax on marijuana and income tax from the many citizens working in the marijuana industry.

You might be thinking, "Wait, that's more than one sentence." Although high-school teachers frequently tell their students to cram the entire thesis into a single sentence, they usually do so because they're trying to help their students stay focused on a narrow topic. However, in a college academic essay, well-crafted and specific thesis statements are often two to four sentences long.

Note, too, that the first sentence in the thesis statement comfortably fits into our Topic + Comment = Thesis Statement formula:

Topic (Legalizing Marijuana) + Comment (Will Improve Our Economy)
= Thesis Statement (Legalizing marijuana will improve our economy.)

"For These Three Reasons ..."

As we've seen repeatedly, moving from high school to higher education involves transitioning to more sophisticated thinking—and phrasing. As you craft your working thesis, do your best to avoid turning it into a simple list.

Admittedly, some instructors will be happy to know that you've at least decided on three main points to cover, but many others will shake their heads and cringe when they see a thesis like "Marijuana should be legalized for these three reasons...."

The thesis-as-numbered-list is one of those academic clichés that you might not yet recognize as a student, but your instructor will be grateful that you avoided it.

State Your Thesis—Don't Announce It

What's the difference between a thesis statement and an announcement? Take a look:

Thesis Statement: Legalizing marijuana will improve our economy.
Announcement: My essay will discuss the legalization of marijuana on our economy.

This may seem like a minor distinction, but the announcement, by neglecting, or refusing, to state a direct opinion ("Legalizing marijuana will improve our economy"), signals that the writer hasn't yet made up his or her mind about how to approach the topic. The announcement is wishy-washy and lifeless.

Don't be afraid to take a stand in your thesis. You reader will appreciate the fact that you have an actual point of view.

Recap: Strong Thesis Statements

Even if the number of words you generate when writing your thesis seems disproportionally small compared to the amount of time you've spent, remember that without a solid thesis, your paper is all but doomed. On the other hand, if you begin with a solid thesis, you will always have a handy "roadmap" to refer back to, which is especially important when you're pressed for time.

As you look over your working thesis, check to see that it meets the following criteria. A strong thesis statement

- is arguable;
- is worth arguing;
- is specific;
- includes a "topic" and a "comment";
- answers a question, whether specifically asked or implied;
- is a statement, not an announcement;
- isn't afraid to take a stand.

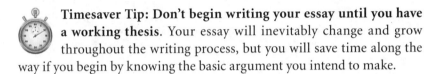 **Timesaver Tip: Don't begin writing your essay until you have a working thesis.** Your essay will inevitably change and grow throughout the writing process, but you will save time along the way if you begin by knowing the basic argument you intend to make.

OUTLINES

As you have already seen, the more specific the thesis, the easier it is for you to identify what you must do to defend it. Indeed, probably the most important test of a thesis is whether or not you can generate enough evidence to support it. An idea might initially look very promising, but once you begin outlining it, you realize that there's really only one main point and you just have one piece of evidence to support that one main point. If nothing else, an outline is a confirmation, or a warning, about how easy it will be to develop substantial body paragraphs.

Traditional Outline

You've probably made a traditional outline at least once in your academic career. This type of outline is linear in nature; it helps you identify your main points, your sub-points, and then shows where evidence will be required to support those points.

Begin your outline with your thesis statement, so that as you write you can look back and make sure you are still on track. The main points and sub-points are usually shown in indented form, with numerical or alphabetical headings, like this:

1. Main Point
    a. Sub-point
        i. Evidence

For our essay, the formatting is along these lines:

1. Larger Topic
    a. Paragraph Topic
        i. Evidence to Support Paragraph

An initial outline on the topic of legalizing marijuana for economic reasons might look like this:

Working Thesis: Legalizing marijuana will improve our economy. Legalization will eliminate the need for costly enforcement of marijuana laws. It will also reduce the expense of building and maintaining prisons because fewer people will be incarcerated. Our government will not only save money, but will also collect revenue through sales tax on marijuana and income tax from the many citizens working in the marijuana industry.

1. Introduction
    a. Hook: Description of the way money is currently being wasted?
    b. Overview of topic
    c. Thesis
2. Reduces costs of prosecuting offenders
    a. Law enforcement
        i. Find *recent* source indicating how much money it costs to hire officers and prosecute crimes
    b. Prisons
        i. Find source on cost of housing marijuana offenders
3. Increases tax revenue for government
    a. Sales tax on marijuana
        i. Find a legitimate economist (Ivy League professor?) predicting how much money marijuana sales will bring in
    b. Income tax from workers in marijuana industry
        i. List all the jobs likely to be created by it—Look at Washington state and Colorado
        ii. Find source showing how much income tax that would create
        iii. Maybe look into something about other ways employed people contribute to the economy? Paying for food, shelter, recreation, etc.

4. Conclusion
   a. Catchy quotation about pot from an unlikely source? A cop maybe?
   b. Talk about how, in tough economic times, the government cannot
      afford to lose so much potential money

What we have here is a **scratch outline**, a rough guide to the essay's
overall structure using words and phrases rather than complete sentences. A
scratch outline doesn't need to include all the details in order to be a useful
guide. After all, the essay is still very much a work-in-progress.

Hierarchical Chart

For those writers who are more spatially oriented, charts provide a clearer
overview of an essay than traditional outlines. One of the most useful charts
is the hierarchical chart. The drawback is that you can't be nearly as detailed
as in a traditional outline. However, the entire essay is laid out so that as
you write, you can keep checking that you're always supporting the top box,
which is your thesis, while staying focused on whichever area you're covering
at the moment. Figure 4.3 shows a hierarchical chart for our proposed essay.

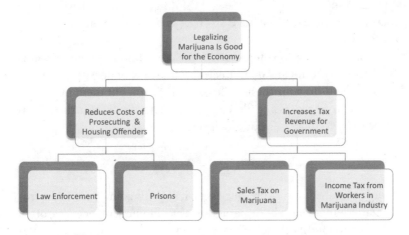

Figure 4.3   *Hierarchical Chart for Essay on Legalizing Marijuana*

CONSIDERING OTHER PERSPECTIVES

Ultimately, in an academic essay, you want to defend and support the point
you set out to argue. However, you also want to be fair-minded in your
consideration of your topic. Remember Aristotle's *ethos*: establishing your
credibility is key to persuading skeptical readers.

Because you are time-bound when writing your essay, it's helpful to start with a particular point of view. However, as you research and write about your topic, you may well come to believe something entirely different. Perhaps, for instance, you discover that the evils of marijuana are far greater than you'd thought, and you need to start over from the opposite perspective, or abandon your topic altogether and find a new one.

Whatever stance you take on an issue, at some point in your final draft you will want to acknowledge the arguments of the other side and address them in a logical, coherent manner. Indeed, your instructor might suggest that you include an entire paragraph devoted to possible counterarguments by those who disagree with you.

Typically, though, it is more effective to raise those counterarguments within a paragraph devoted to one of your main points. In body paragraph 2 on the costs of imprisoning drug felons, for instance, you might write, "Granted, the majority of people serving time for drug possession were arrested for marijuana. However, the number of those in jail for having relatively small amounts of pot is surprisingly high."

In short, as you proceed with your research, don't ignore evidence that contradicts your beliefs. Instead, take careful note of it, then—if it doesn't sway you to change your opinion—begin thinking of ways to prove that the evidence on your side of the issue is stronger and more persuasive.

Timesaver Tip: As you research your topic, take notes on opinions different than your own. Keep careful track of possible counterarguments to your thesis. Then, whether you put them in a paper file folder, or a word processing file, or simply in a notebook, save these ideas in a single place to increase your efficiency.

TOPIC SENTENCES

Once you've finished outlining your essay, it's worth going back and turning the main point of each body paragraph into a topic sentence. Yes, often you will need to modify these sentences as you compose your essay, just as you may need to modify your thesis itself. However, beginning the writing process with a solid idea of what you want to accomplish in each body paragraph will help focus those paragraphs and nearly always save you time in the long run.

Students occasionally worry that—as with a clear and forceful thesis statement—a well-defined topic sentence at the beginning of the paragraph is too "obvious." And it's true that not every paragraph in every academic essay will begin with, or even necessarily include, a traditional topic sentence.

That said, most instructors are busy people, and they appreciate these clear markers or "signposts" showing where the writer plans to go. A good topic sentence makes a promise: this paragraph will be about this subject, and a good paragraph keeps that promise by always supporting the topic sentence.

Our initial thesis statement—"Legalizing marijuana will improve our economy"—is followed by the four main points we plan to cover in the first draft. With just a bit of revision, those elements of the thesis can be transformed into topic sentences:

Topic Sentence 1: Legalization will eliminate the need for the costly enforcement of marijuana laws.

Topic Sentence 2: Legalization will also reduce the expense of building and maintaining prisons because fewer people will be incarcerated.

Topic Sentence 3: Our government will not only save money, but will also collect revenue by taxing marijuana sales.

Topic Sentence 4: In addition to the revenue provided through sales tax, the government will also receive income tax from the many citizens working in the marijuana industry.

Well-marked transitions at the beginning of each new paragraph make for easy reading, and they reassure your reader that you have a clear overall plan for your essay's structure. Note the basic but effective transition words and phrases in the final three body paragraphs:

Topic Sentence 2: Legalization **will also.**...

Topic Sentence 3: Our government **will not only** save money, but **will also.**...

Topic Sentence 4: **In addition to** the revenue provided....

Certainly, you want to be flexible with your outline. If, as you write, you realize your essay is not turning out the way you'd hoped, you'll want to revise your thesis and re-sketch the plan for your essay. It's not unusual for an entire paragraph to be crossed out because of lack of evidence or inconsistent support for the thesis.

Moreover, as we've already noted, every writer is different: there is no single way to structure an academic essay that is going to work perfectly for everyone. Nevertheless, you can see that it helps significantly to begin with a 1) clear thesis statement, 2) a working outline, and 3) topic sentences for each paragraph. A little time invested before you begin writing your essay can save you hours of flailing around for a focus during the drafting process.

Timesaver Tip: Turn off your phone. Have you ever picked up your phone when you've been struggling with a difficult passage of reading, or you've reached a temporary roadblock in your writing? We all do it, thinking we deserve a short break, that some texting or a few minutes of web surfing will help us relax and refocus. Occasionally, that's true, of course, but far more often, grabbing your phone simply postpones the completion of necessary hard work. The next time you sit down to do some academic reading and writing, see how much more productive you are if your phone is powered off—or is at least in the other room.

Questions and Suggestions FOR You

1. Share your essay topic with another student or a friend and have that person list as many questions as possible about your topic. Answer the question you find most intriguing, with the goal of generating a thesis in response to that question.
2. Craft a working thesis statement for your essay. When you're finished, reread it and make sure it contains an argument and is not simply a statement of fact.
3. Make sure your thesis contains both a topic *and* a comment: a statement of what you intend to discuss as well as how you will approach the subject matter.
4. Ask yourself if your thesis is sufficiently narrow for the essay you have been assigned to write. Even if your professor encourages "big thinking," don't write about more than you can comfortably handle in the number of pages you have been assigned.
5. Write a traditional outline for your essay. Then write a hierarchical outline, using either a pencil and paper or the SmartArt (or similar) feature on your word-processing program. As you begin drafting your essay, which outline do you find yourself turning to more frequently? Your answer will probably dictate which type of outline you choose to write in the future.
6. Using your thesis statement and your outline as guides, write out your topic sentences as *complete sentences*. Imagine that each sentence will begin one of your body paragraphs.

Questions and Suggestions FROM You

List three questions you still have after reading this section. Start by reviewing the chapter. If that method doesn't inspire three questions, think about the overall topic of generating a focus for your essay. What don't you know about arguments and organization that you would still like to know?

1. _____

_____

_____

_____

_____

2. _____

_____

_____

_____

_____

3. _____

_____

_____

_____

_____

Describe one activity related to writing thesis statements and outlines *not mentioned in this chapter* that you think would be helpful to do in class. Any successful activity in any course you've ever taken might serve as a model.

_____

_____

_____

_____

_____

CHAPTER FIVE

Researching Your Topic

THE **CARS** CHECKLIST
LIBRARY DATABASES
BOOKS
INTERNET SOURCES

In years past, research meant long trips to the library, thumbing through bound volumes of periodicals at a lonely desk while fluorescent lights flickered overhead. The air was stuffy, and if you were brazen enough to try and sneak in some food or drink, a librarian was probably waiting around the corner to send you packing.

These days, of course, most libraries are nothing like that and students are at least as likely to interact with a librarian through an electronic chat as they are in person. Moreover, the word "research" is now often used very differently than it once was. "Have you bought those concert tickets?" you might hear someone say, with the other person replying, "Not yet. I'm researching the best available seats."

In fact, if you think of research as the sort of thing you already do all the time, it doesn't actually sound very intimidating. That's good because writing academic essays requires a keen and persistent investigative mind, and you're likely to be researching your topic throughout the writing of your essay. Indeed, an academic essay without any research at all is just a collection of unsubstantiated opinions—a sure-fire recipe for a lousy grade.

To help you concentrate your energy and efforts, this chapter covers some of the most frequently used research techniques, with a particular emphasis on using library databases. We'll also look at why simply typing a few words into Google and cutting and pasting from the first result that appears is not what most professors consider "research."

Yes, solid research does sometimes require more time—but no more time than some people spend looking for the best price on a pair of shoes. And researching isn't always time-intensive, especially with the help of librarians. Often, it's simply a matter of looking in new and more reliable places.

THE CARS CHECKLIST

As we saw in Chapter 3, most students—and, let's face it, professors, too—begin investigating a topic by going online. Therefore, while we'll talk briefly about print sources, the focus of this chapter is web-based research.

The transition from print to digital hasn't been an easy one, and online sources present a special problem for college students. While many are excellent, some are, to use the phrase of a colleague of mine, "unmitigated crap." There's no single method for insuring that every source you use is valid, but many college and university librarians recommend "the CARS Checklist" when evaluating online sources. CARS stands for:

1. Credibility
2. Accuracy
3. Reasonableness
4. Support

Basically, the checklist is a series of questions that you ask about a source, particularly one you find through a general Internet search. You can refer back to the CARS checklist throughout the writing process, and while it is primarily meant for online research, it applies equally well to print sources.

Credibility

Is the source primarily academic, or commercial? Though domain names are no guarantee of credibility (or lack thereof), those ending in .org, .gov, and .edu tend, overall, to be more credible than those ending in .com.

Does the source list an author or authors? We've grown so used to reading websites that don't have an author listed that we sometimes don't think to check for an author at all. However, academic research is based on work done by people who *want* to take credit for their hard work. If it's impossible to tell who wrote what you are reading, you probably want to look elsewhere.

If the author is named, are her or his credentials listed? Anyone can post anything online, so simply putting your name at the top or bottom of an article doesn't mean you are a credible author. Often, an academic author's name is linked to a university website, and you can generally get a pretty good sense of his or her accomplishments from that source. If you're at all doubtful, though, it's a good idea to run a separate search yourself. If, for instance, an author says she's an economics professor at Harvard, do you find her listed on the Economics Department website?

If the author seems reliable, are his or her credentials relevant to your essay? That Harvard economist might be a fantastic source for a paper on the Great Recession of 2009, but if your essay is about the nutritional value of fermented pickles in rural Ontario, wouldn't another source be more suitable?

Bottom line: If you want your reader to trust your source, the source needs to be named, trustworthy, and appropriate to the research you are doing.

Accuracy

When was the last time the source was updated? The quicker a field changes, the more important it is to have timely information. Computer-based technology, for instance, can shift overnight. An article published in 2007 about the attributes of the iPhone would be woefully inadequate as a source on the latest version.

If there is no date, would a lack of timeliness affect the validity of the source? A website featuring primary historical sources—the transcript of a nineteenth-century speech or the text of the Constitution, for example—wouldn't necessarily need to be updated as frequently as a technology website. However, *interpretations* of history are changing all the time, even if the documents they are based on remain the same. If a website has not been updated in years—if it looks like the online equivalent of a long-neglected garden—you may want to turn elsewhere for your information.

Is the source vague? The more specific the information, the easier it is to check the truthfulness of a source. Look for sources that showcase concrete details and precise language; avoid the general, the ambiguous, and the incomplete.

Bottom line: The more recent and specific your source, the more likely it will be useful evidence for your argument.

Reasonableness

Is the source fair, objective, moderate, and consistent? While individual commentators on the Canadian Broadcasting Corporation (CBC) and National Public Radio (NPR) may occasionally betray biases, these two national radio networks make a concerted effort to cover all sides of the important issues in their respective countries. Reasonable sources value their reputations for making considered, rational judgments, and they work hard to maintain those reputations.

Does the source make exaggerated or sweeping statements? Yes, sometimes one point of view seems very wrong or very right, but the truth can generally be found somewhere in the middle. If a source is given to the sort of pronouncements you might hear in a loud bar or at a sporting event, beware.

If the source seems biased, does that bias appear to be interfering with the truth? No source is entirely bias-free, but some news organizations, for example, clearly favor a particular political point of view. Sources like the *Huffington Post* and MSNBC lean to the left, while FoxNews and townhall.com lean right. Supporting one side or the other of an issue doesn't necessarily mean a writer can't be accurate, but you should be extra careful when referencing potentially partisan information.

Bottom line: A source that attempts to transcend bias and always hear both sides of a story is generally one that can be trusted.

Support

Is the material supported by a Works Cited page or some other documentation? We are all entitled to our opinions, but those opinions are generally useless as secondary sources for an academic essay unless they are supported by verifiable evidence.

Can the evidence provided by the source be corroborated by another source? The more frequently a source is substantiated and appears in print or on credible websites, the more likely you should trust it. If, however, an unsubstantiated claim only appears on one website, or if the same claim appears elsewhere, but never with any evidence to back it up, be wary.

Can the source be contacted if you would like to verify its information? A professor who makes a claim about climate change can be contacted via email, as can a news organization that reports a story about elder abuse. Obviously, you can't communicate with the deceased and missing, but you should be able to find out who has posted their work.

Bottom line: Just as your instructor is actively assessing the validity of the works you cite, you should be assessing the authority of your own sources.

As you've been reading through the questions in the CARS Checklist, you've no doubt realized that it emphasizes certain traits that college students doing research should possess:

- *Skepticism*: there's more bad information out there than good: if something seems sketchy, it probably is;
- *Pride*: every source you cite represents the quality of your thinking—citing unsatisfactory sources makes you look like an inadequate thinker;
- *Honesty*: trying to pass off a weak source as a legitimate one not only makes you appear less than sharp, but it can also make you seem dishonest;
- *Precision*: double-check your sources and cite them accurately (see Appendix II for details).

LIBRARY DATABASES

Often the best place to do an initial search for sources is your college or university's library database. Unlike a general search engine such as Google, which draws on a vast range of sources, many of them questionable and/or driven primarily by profit, most of the sources in your library's database have already been vetted by career scholars and professional editors.

Indeed, one of the reasons library databases tend to be more reliable is that the profit motive has already been addressed: libraries pay to subscribe to massive databases like EBSCOhost and ProQuest, and the material accessed in scholarly journals is mostly ad-free. Library home pages normally include instructions for making the most of your research efforts, and librarians can help you navigate into the most relevant set of databases.

To focus our discussion in this chapter, let's imagine the essay topic you are researching is physician-assisted dying for terminally ill patients. Like any hot-button topic, this one will have vociferous proponents and detractors, which makes beginning our research in a library database a good idea. Certainly we will be hearing strong opinions, but at least in the scholarly journals we search, we know those opinions will be supported by solid evidence.

Often our opinions on a topic such as this one are informed by personal experience. Let's say your grandfather suffered a years-long decline from Alzheimer's disease. By the time of his death, he could no longer speak, move, or even eat without a feeding tube. You were close to him, and the experience left you with strong feelings in favor of physician-assisted dying.

Boolean Operators

Taking just a few minutes to read through the search instructions on a database will save time later on, so, rather than simply typing in your search, slow down long enough to figure out how the database works.

One easy way to search efficiently is to use the **Boolean operators**: AND, OR, NOT or AND NOT. The nineteenth-century British mathematician George Boole developed a system of including or excluding items retrieved from a list, and his pre-web logic has turned out to work wonders in search engines.

Boolean operators function in different ways on different databases. Sometimes they need to be capitalized, and sometimes the search terms need to be in quotation marks or parentheses. Their basic functions, however, are as follows:

AND: Both items in the search will be retrieved. **This narrows your search**. If you were to use "physician assisted" AND "dying," for example, your search would return only results that included BOTH terms. Use AND if you are receiving too many results.

OR: Either or both terms will be retrieved. **This expands your search**. This time, "physician assisted" OR "dying" would expand your results to include pages that *might* be related to your topic, but might not. Use OR if you are receiving too few results.

NOT or AND NOT: The first term will be searched but the second term will be excluded. **This significantly narrows your search**. Suppose, for instance, that you did not want any results related to Dr. Jack Kevorkian, the most famous activist in the realm of physician-assisted dying. You would type "physician-assisted dying" AND NOT "Kevorkian." Different databases will respond best to one or the other of these terms, but both basically exclude an item you do not want to see but would otherwise normally be retrieved.

Types of Database Searches

Most databases allow you to search in both advanced and basic modes. The three most common types of searches are keyword, subject, and field:

Keyword Search: Databases typically open in "basic mode." A single search box allows you to type in a keyword or phrase associated with your topic, which is normally matched against the entire database. While you may receive results that don't necessarily apply to your essay's focus, a keyword search will give you a sense of the current conversation taking place on your topic. Searching our topic, for example, you will quickly notice that the word "suicide" occurs more frequently than "dying." This is a helpful bit of information because it allows you to more successfully research your topic, and it betrays a bias in the discussion. "Dying," after all, is normal: we all do it. "Suicide," by contrast, is considered a sin by many religions, and attempted suicide is against the law in some countries.

Subject Search: Usually you see the available subject headings after typing in a keyword search. In EBSCOhost, for instance, typing in "physician-assisted dying" returns several thousand results, many of which include the subject heading "Assisted Suicide." Typing "Assisted Suicide" into the database brings in almost twice as many results, and provides a number of possible sub-topics worth investigating: "Assisted Suicide—Law & Legislation," "Assisted Suicide—Moral & Ethical Aspects," "Assisted Suicide—Decision Making," "Assisted Suicide—Patient Education," and so on.

Field Search: A field search allows you to look for material by title, date, type of publication, topic, author, and so on. Often the field search is accessed through an "Advanced Search" link. While you can be much more precise in the investigation of your topic with a field search, you obviously wouldn't use this function until you were somewhat familiar with your topic.

Scholarly Journals

Scholarly articles can be the backbone of an outstanding academic essay, and you should generally turn to them first to ensure that you have quality research in your paper. **Scholarly journals** are "peer-reviewed" or "refereed," which means the contents have been evaluated by other experts in the field: they are the opposite of blogs. Whereas just about anyone is capable of writing and posting on a blog, hardly anyone is qualified to publish in a prestigious scholarly journal. The work in scholarly journals tends to be cutting-edge and supported by plentiful hard evidence. Unlike **newspapers**, which are published daily, or **popular periodicals**, which are published on a weekly or monthly basis and are intended for a general audience, scholarly journals are published only several times a year for their small, but highly educated and very demanding, audiences.

For most students, of course, this isn't the sort of material to unwind with after a long day at school. The titles of journals publishing articles on physician-assisted suicide, for example, have names like *Palliative Medicine*; *The Journal of Law, Medicine & Ethics*; and *The International Journal of Law & Psychiatry*. However, the very specificity and seriousness of the journal titles are an indication of the specificity and seriousness of their contents.

Because the articles are written for professionals in the field—peers of the authors—reading these journals can be hard work. Here are four tips for making your way through the often dense contents of a scholarly journal:

- *Read the title carefully.* The first article that pops up may not be the one you need or want. Indeed, you may have to skim through pages of results to find what you are looking for. Titles are the quickest way to assess the article's content.
- *Read the abstract first (but don't quote from it).* Scholarly articles normally begin with an **abstract**, a brief summary of the article's contents. Read the abstract carefully, but don't quote from it in your essay. (An abstract may be written by the journal's editors rather than the author.) Instead, if the author makes a point you agree with, find the corresponding section in the article and quote from that passage instead.
- *Don't worry if you don't understand everything.* Unless you're an expert in the field, you probably *shouldn't* understand all the **jargon**, or specialized speech, in a scholarly article. You should, however, be able to discern the author's overall argument, and recognize quotable moments within the article.
- *Save the article.* If you find a useful quotation, you will need to summarize the article for the quotation to make sense and have its fullest impact. Print out the article, link to it, or save it on your computer, but *don't lose it.* You will need quick access when you are drafting your essay and again when you are documenting your source in a Works Cited page.

Let's take an example from our EBSCOhost search of how you might use an article from a scholarly journal. One of the items returned is by a British physician named Phillip A. Berry. It appears in Volume 8, Issue 1, of the journal *Clinical Ethics* and is entitled "From Empathy to Assisted Dying: An

Argument." The abstract reveals that Dr. Berry believes a responsible doctor should prioritize respect for a patient's "autonomy above legal or societal objections." Reading through the article with an eye for a sentence or two that succinctly expresses that belief, we find the following lines in the conclusion, on page 8: "Through empathy we begin to experience the patient's situation and are better able to help them. If they desire death, and that desire is sustained, we must reach the conclusion that death is the best outcome for them."

We'll talk more in Chapter 7 about how to document quotations and situate them in a paragraph, but for now we can quickly rearrange this material so that it is ready for later use:

> Writing in the journal *Clinical Ethics*, British physician Phillip A. Berry maintains that a responsible doctor should put his patient's interests above those of society and the law. In "From Empathy to Assisted Dying: An Argument," Dr. Berry argues that "Through empathy we begin to experience the patient's situation and are better able to help them. If they desire death, and that desire is sustained, we must reach the conclusion that death is the best outcome for them" (8).

Newspapers and Popular Periodicals

Library databases usually allow you to select the source type you want to search. If scholarly journals are the first stop in your research process, popular periodicals can provide a user-friendly follow-up.

You'll want to gravitate toward those periodicals that have been around for a while and have demonstrated a commitment to accuracy and integrity. Among the major North American newspapers are the *Globe and Mail*, the *Los Angeles Times*, the *New York Times*, *La Presse*, the *Toronto Star*, the *Wall Street Journal*, and the *Washington Post*. Major newsmagazines include the *Atlantic*, *Maclean's*, the *New Yorker*, and *Time*. Your library database will also retrieve results from a number of smaller, but still reliable, periodicals, although the smaller and more specialized the popular periodical, the more likely it will be subject to a pronounced editorial bias.

A search on our topic in popular periodicals returns an article by Cathy Gulu published in the March 3, 2014, edition of *Maclean's* entitled "Closing Arguments: Controversial and Complex, Canada's End-of-Life Debate Is Coming to a Head." Gulu's article covers a town hall-style meeting held in St. John's, Newfoundland. Unlike the author of a scholarly journal, who is an academic or professional speaking out on his or her subject of expertise, Gulu is a reporter whose primary goal is to document what experts said at the meeting.

The *Maclean's* article doesn't have the professorial tone of the article in *Clinical Ethics*; in other words, Gulu's piece is much easier to read. "Closing Arguments" yields a very persuasive quotation from a doctor in favor of physician-assisted dying. Greg Robinson, a retired epidemiologist from Toronto, tells Gulu: "I don't take it away from anybody who wants to be stoic at the end of life—by all means, be stoic. But don't enforce your values upon me.... If I choose because of my suffering that this is the end, and I want to be with my family and friends in a loving way and say goodbye rather than flailing around in pain and agony, then offer me that opportunity." (Note: Because the article appears in html, not pdf, format, there is no page number to cite.)

Once again, even though you aren't yet certain how you will use this information, it will save you time later on if you contextualize the quotation before moving on to your next source. Using the example from the scholarly journal above, see if you can craft the information from *Maclean's* into a similar quotation. You will need to include the following information:

The title of the journal + the title of the article + the author's name + a brief summary of the article + a quotation from the article.

_____

_____

_____

_____

_____

Online Encyclopedias

Providing a subject overview, the function of general encyclopedias, like the old *Encyclopedia Britannica*, has been taken over mostly by Wikipedia (see below). General encyclopedias *are* often quoted by third-graders writing their very first papers, but in college you should steer away from them as citable sources.

In contrast, specialty encyclopedias provide a more scholarly summary of the main issues in a field. Many of these encyclopedias contain not only general articles on a topic, but also links to the sources on which the articles are based. We might, for example, turn to the medical encyclopedia *Med-*

linePlus for help with our topic. This source points us toward insightful and well-documented articles published by the Alzheimer's Association and the National Institute of Health.

Timesaver Tip: Begin your research in your library's database. We are creatures of habit, and if Google is your home page, you will probably begin your research there without even thinking. Remember, though, that your library's database contains material that is peer-reviewed or published by an established newspaper or periodical. Don't waste your time sorting through junk on the web when you can immediately get to the good stuff via a database. And don't hesitate to contact a librarian if you need help.

BOOKS

Finding relevant books for your essay is a hit-or-miss proposition. A good book on your topic can truly bring it to life. The author will likely have spent years researching and writing about the topic, and you will find quotations galore for your essay.

On the other hand, relying too heavily on books can be a problem. Because knowledge is being generated much faster than it was just a few decades ago, books on topics like physician-assisted dying go out of date much sooner than they used to.

Moreover, access to books can be a problem. If you attend a large research university, your library may be many stories tall, and so full of books you can get lost wandering among the stacks. On the other hand, small and community college libraries generally have fewer resources. College librarians with limited annual budgets may well choose to spend that money on databases, which can be quite expensive.

Interlibrary Loan

Fortunately, whatever the size of your institution, you will probably have access to interlibrary loan, which allows colleges and universities to pool their collective resources, vastly expanding the number of titles available to students. Interlibrary loan is also usually free.

That's the upside. The downside is that it can take anywhere from a few days to a couple of weeks for borrowed books to arrive at your home library. If you're the sort of student who begins work on an essay the moment it is assigned, interlibrary loan is a great tool. However, if you're down to your last 48 hours before the due date, this service won't be of much use.

Browsing the Stacks

If you are lucky enough to have a large research library at your disposal, you'll find that browsing the stacks, a pastime of generations of college students, can be an effective way to find information.

Simply identify the Library of Congress or Dewey Decimal system number for your topic, and head for the books. (For example, the Library of Congress number for our topic is R726, while the Dewey Decimal system number is 179.)

Often a book with a fantastic-sounding title doesn't have anything to do with your essay. In contrast, the book you'd dismissed while skimming the online listings turns out to be just what you were looking for.

Deciding which books to check out of the library doesn't require reading the entire book, of course. Here are a few tips:

- **Flip through the book quickly**, looking for words, phrases, or images that you recognize.
- **Read the table of contents**, and then follow up by paging to any sections that look particularly promising.
- If you have a fairly clear idea of your topic already, **check out keywords in the alphabetical index at the back of the book**. If those keywords are present, skim the appropriate pages in the book for information that supports your thesis.

Even if the book only ends up supplying you with one strong idea or one solid quotation, it's worth checking out of the library. And even if you don't find a book for your essay, all that browsing will have made you more knowledgeable about your topic.

Google Books and Amazon Previews

In 2004, Google declared that it intended to digitize 15 million print books. These books were not just those in the public domain—that is, they could legally be reproduced for free—but also those that were copyright-protected.

Not surprisingly, the web giant caused a great outcry among authors and publishers who intended to sell their work for profit. If all books were free on Google, why would anyone ever *buy* a book again?

A legal saga followed—one that might make for an interesting research paper—but the upshot is that Google Books is a far from perfect resource. Searching for "physician-assisted dying" brings up a number of books published in the last century, as well as books that only allow for a limited "preview," meaning that some, many, or most of the pages are not available for viewing.

Google Books does provide information that you might have trouble finding elsewhere. Long out-of-print books may be reproduced in full on this site. However, prepare to be frustrated if you rely too heavily on this source.

A similarly erratic, but occasionally valuable, resource is Amazon.com. The advantage of an Amazon over a Google Books preview is that Amazon tends to give viewers access to more current books. Amazon, of course, wants you to buy the books it sells, but in order to do so, it often provides free previews of their contents. Some previews show only the first few pages, but a surprising number of books include a majority of the book's contents. The problem is that, in order to encourage viewers to purchase the book, Amazon frequently withholds key pages, so you can never be quite certain what you're missing.

It is difficult to do thorough research on either Google Books or through Amazon previews. Nevertheless, if you have already done the bulk of your work and are simply looking for one final pithy quotation, these sources can be useful.

INTERNET SOURCES

Much of what I've already said about searching library databases applies to Internet searches too: 1) Know what you're looking for, but 2) be open to interesting surprises.

There is, of course, one huge difference: no one has gone through and vetted the material in a Google search for CARS: Credibility, Accuracy, Reasonableness, and Support. In fact, the majority of search results returned will be unusable for an academic essay.

Especially if your instructor has been teaching for any length of time, he or she will be extremely tired of reading academic essays "supported" by the flimsiest of evidence from dubious sources. Do yourself and your professor a favor and don't rely on patently unconvincing information from websites that no reasonable person would trust.

Avoid This Common Error: Relying on websites aimed primarily at students writing essays. If a commercial website seems primarily directed toward students searching for sources that can be crammed into an essay at the last minute, look elsewhere. You'll know these "sources" by their flashing advertisements, anonymous authors, and general resemblance to sleazy motels.

Google Scholar

While the World Wide Web remains the World *Wild* Web in many respects, there *are* places where you can locate peer-reviewed material. Google Scholar is similar to a library database, but with a generally smaller percentage of free and full-text articles. Google Scholar is often buried fairly deep down on the list of Google options and is sometimes hard to find (if you don't see it, you can always Google it).

A search on the topic of "physician-assisted suicide"—by now we've come to see that this is the preferred term for most articles—returns a number of intriguing sources, but, like Google Books, Google Scholar provides a sometimes frustrating experience. An article in the scholarly journal *Annals of Internal Medicine*, for instance, is available only to subscribers. An article in the prestigious *New England Journal of Medicine* is helpful, but, again, a significant amount of information on the topic can be accessed only by subscription.

The Internet Public Library

The Internet Public Library is a nonprofit website that now includes the resources of the Librarians Internet Index. Hosted at Drexel University, the IPL does not have the resources of your college's library database, but it is free and easily accessible.

Wikipedia

Wikipedia doesn't quite have the anti-academic reputation it once did, although many professors still discourage students from citing it in an academic essay.

One of the reasons you'll want to avoid quoting from Wikipedia articles is because—unlike a scholarly article or book—their content changes so often. Granted, these changes are generally for the better, but you never know if some of the information is inaccurate. You can see all the changes ever made to an entry by clicking on "View history" at the top of a Wikipedia page, and you may be surprised how often an important topic gets changed—occasionally, when big things are happening, many times in a single day.

Right next to the "View" link is "Edit," and while Wikipedia is far more scrupulous than it used to be about who can edit material and when that material will go live, there is still room for shenanigans—Wikipedia has been the victim of a number of hoaxes.

Another reason to be wary of Wikipedia is the fact that the quality of the articles varies so dramatically. Certainly, many articles are well researched and carefully written. Many more articles, however, are "stubs"—largely undocumented and very brief.

Still, reading the Wikipedia entry on your topic does have several potential benefits:

- It can give you a quick overview of your topic, even if that overview is flawed.
- If an article is well-documented, it will provide links to primary and secondary sources for you to access on your own.
- Wikipedia articles tend to be very up-to-the-minute (although sometimes, unfortunately, information is posted before it has been independently verified).

Online Interviews

While the Internet certainly has its limitations when looking for authoritative secondary sources, it is a good place to go for primary sources, particularly interviews. A quick Google search on our topic returns not only print interviews, but several interesting interviews with doctors posted on YouTube. For instance, an interview with Dutch doctor Bert Keizer on the website of his publisher, Random House, is brief yet eloquent. Another page links to an Anderson Cooper interview on CNN with "Dr. Death," Jack Kevorkian. Both these sources are credible and quote-worthy.

Nevertheless, the further you go from the safety of scholarly, peer-reviewed sources, the more likely you are to cite a source your instructor won't find credible. Think of a general Internet search as something you do *after* you've completed more scholarly research.

Avoid This Common Error: Skimming the surface. After you have gathered your initial research, look back over it and ask yourself, "Do I really *understand* my topic?" Normally, the act of reading extensively about your subject—especially when you have already written an intelligent working thesis and outline—will lead to at least a serviceable understanding of your material. However, if you are simply skimming through articles as fast as possible in search of quotations, you may be missing crucial elements of the conversation.

To make sure you really know what you're talking about, take a few minutes to tell a friend or relative about the subject of your essay. Encourage that person to ask you questions. If you can't answer them, reread your sources more slowly and carefully to ensure you are, if not an expert, at least someone who is more knowledgeable about the topic than the average person.

Questions and Suggestions FOR You

1. Search for your topic on your library's database, focusing first on the resources in scholarly journals, and then on well-respected general-interest magazines and newspapers.
2. Run a general Internet search on your topic. Use the CARS test to identify the most reliable sources.
3. Write a paragraph comparing and contrasting the Credibility, Accuracy, Reasonableness, and Support of the strongest scholarly journal source with your strongest Internet source. What are the relative advantages and disadvantages of each one?
4. Search your topic on Google Books and Google Scholar. Try and find at least one quotation from each source that might serve as evidence to support your argument.
5. Look up your topic on Wikipedia. After reviewing the entry, locate the sources used to write the article and determine if any of them might be helpful in the composition of your essay.
6. Review your assignment to find out how many sources are required for your essay, and then look over all the research you have gathered so far. Ask yourself these questions: Which sources are keepers? What else do you still need to learn? Where can you find that missing information?
7. Spend some time with your college or university librarian locating sources you still need to complete your initial research and assessing any sources you worry might be weak.

Questions and Suggestions FROM You

List three questions you still have after reading this section. Start by reviewing the chapter. If that method doesn't inspire three questions, think about the overall topic of research. What don't you know about academic research that you would still like to know?

1. _____

_____

_____

_____

_____

2. _____

_____

_____

_____

_____

3. _____

_____

_____

_____

_____

Describe one activity related to academic research *not mentioned in this chapter* that you think would be helpful to do in class. Any successful activity in any course you've ever taken might serve as a model.

_____

_____

_____

_____

_____

PART TWO: GO

CHAPTER SIX

Introduction: Hooking Your Reader

While you will want to have a working thesis when you begin drafting your essay, the introductory paragraph may not be the first paragraph you write. You might even write your opening paragraph after you've completed the rest of your essay. However, your introduction *will* be the first thing your readers read, so we'll discuss it first, as though it were the initial step in your essay-drafting process. Besides drawing in the reader, introductions to academic essays usually provide a brief overview of the essay topic and end with a thesis statement.

On the positive side, this structure allows you to move quickly into the heart of your essay. Because it is familiar to you and your professor, it ensures that both writer and reader are, literally, on the same page.

The negative aspect of the standard introductory paragraph is that it is *overly* familiar. It's easy to think of this as simply another box to be checked off on the way to completing one more uninspiring essay.

That's a mistake, of course. You might wonder whether introductions deserve an entire chapter in a short book like this one, but making a positive first impression on your reader gains you significant good will for the rest of the paper, just as a weak opening may make your reader dread the remainder of your essay.

OPENING SENTENCES

When they market homes, realtors are always concerned with "curb appeal," how a house looks when you see it from the street. The best homes have a "wow factor," something unusually appealing that makes a potential buyer eager to come inside and explore the property. A strong first impression often leads to a sale.

Granted, you are a writer, not a realtor, but you are "marketing" your essay to your instructor, and there's no better place to make a strong initial impression than your very first sentence. Of course professors, like home-buyers, have different tastes. Some prefer a more formal opening, but most instructors of first-year English courses are delighted to be presented with a "wow factor" at the very start.

Put yourself in your professor's place. It's the weekend, and you'd rather be outside riding your bike instead of staring at a stack of essays that need to be graded by Monday. Even worse, experience tells you that many of these essays will be written without much thought as to how you, the professor, will respond. You fear it's going to be a boring couple of days when, *voilà!*— the first paper you pick up has a fantastic opening sentence. Forget about the bike ride: here's an essay that you really want to read.

One of the best ways to see the variety of strategies professional writers employ to "hook" their readers is to read their work. Consider, for example, the thought and creativity that have gone into these opening sentences from essays published in recent volumes of the *Best American Essays*. Each sentence suggests a strategy that other writers might follow.

Tell a Story

Ron Rindo's discussion of his battle with Ménière's disease, "Gyromancy," begins like this: "The external details of this story are well-known: On December 23, 1888, during the first of three unspecified 'attacks' manifested over several months while he lived and painted in Arles, a village in Provence, Vincent Van Gogh sliced off the lower half of his left ear and presented it to a prostitute before being admitted to the local hospital."

It's amazing how much information can be conveyed in a few words: the date of Van Gogh's attack (which was later thought to be caused by Ménière's disease), where it occurred, what he did, what happened to him. Storytelling doesn't have to go on for pages to be effective. In fact, little "stories" like this one of a sentence (or two) can work well not only in your introduction but throughout your essay.

Ask an Intriguing Question

In "Dog Is Our Copilot," her essay on the evolution and breeding of dogs, Kathryn Miles asks, "Could everything we know and love (or hate) about evolution depend upon a singularly pampered Victorian terrier?"

How unlikely, we immediately respond. And yet there must be something to the question if the author has taken the trouble to ask it. Surely the rest of the essay will provide an answer. Opening an academic essay with a question is a time-honored technique, but to open with an *intriguing* question, you must be *specific*. Think of how much would be lost if we changed "singularly pampered Victorian terrier" to the bland catch-all "dog."

Make an Interesting List

"Brooklyn the Unknowable" is Phillip Lopate's tribute to the city where he lives. It begins: "I sing of Brooklyn, the fruited plain, cradle of literary genius and standup comedy, awash in history, relics from Indian mounds, Dutch farms, Revolutionary War battles, breweries and baseball."

Like any interesting list, Lopate's opening sentence includes elements we wouldn't expect to see together: Dutch farms *and* standup comedy? *Really?* Yes, Lopate suggests, there's a lot more to Brooklyn than you thought: read on.

Exaggerate for Comic Effect

Joseph Epstein launches into an essay on boredom, "Duh, Bor-ing," with a list, but this one tests our patience by extending the catalogue of boring things almost to the breaking point: "Unrequited love, as Lorenz Hart instructed us, is a bore, but then so are a great many other things: old friends gone somewhat dotty from whom it is too late to disengage, the important social-science book of the month, 95 percent of the items on the evening news, discussions about the Internet, arguments against the existence of God, people who overestimate their charm, all talk about wine, *New York Times* editorials, lengthy lists (like this one), and, not least, oneself."

Sandra Tsing Loh uses a similar tactic in her essay on menopause, "The Bitch Is Back": "During menopause, a woman can feel like the only way she can continue to exist for ten more seconds inside her crawling, burning skin is to walk screaming into the sea—grandly, epically, and terrifyingly, like a fifteen-foot-tall Greek tragic figure wearing a giant, pop-eyed wooden mask."

Admittedly, some instructors might find such sentences over the top, unsuitable for an academic essay. But if you know your instructor has a sense of humor and play, outrageous gambits like these could be very inviting.

Write a Surprising Declarative Sentence

Here is ophthalmologist John Gamel's opening for "The Elegant Eyeball," a detailed essay about his profession: "They aren't what most people think they are."

In another startling first sentence from a healthcare professional, registered nurse Jane Churchon writes in "The Dead Book": "I like to take my time when I pronounce someone dead."

And James Marcus starts "Faint Music" with this line: "Without a doubt, it's a family affliction." What is a family affliction? (A propensity for fainting, we soon learn.)

All three of these sentences are short, and all insist that you read on to find out exactly what the writer is talking about. Again, what makes these sentences effective is that they are *unexpected*. The least successful lead sentence in an academic essay is the one your instructor is anticipating, the one she or he has read a thousand times before.

Allude to an Outmoded Belief

Alan Lightman begins "The Accidental Universe," an essay on theoretical physics, by referring to long-discarded beliefs about atoms: "In the fifth century B.C.E., the philosopher Democritus proposed that all matter was made of tiny and indivisible atoms, which came in various sizes and textures—some hard and some soft, some smooth and some thorny."

We know now that atoms are nothing like Democritus described them, but this bit of historical detail, and its implication that knowledge is always changing, provides an appealing invitation to a challenging subject.

Forward a Claim That You Intend to Disprove

In "The Crazy State of Psychiatry," an essay on the over-prescription of psychotropic drugs, Marcia Angell writes, "It seems that Americans are in the midst of a raging epidemic of mental illness, at least as it is judged by the increase in the numbers treated for it."

I talked in Chapter 4 about acknowledging the potential counterarguments of those who believe differently than you do. One strategy is to begin straight-out with your opponents' claims, and then get right to work convincing readers your point of view is more valid.

Provide the Quotation That Triggered the Writing of Your Essay

"Only a sentence, casually placed as a footnote in the back of Justin Kaplan's thick 2003 biography of Walt Whitman, but it goes off like a little explosion: 'Bram Stoker based the character of Dracula on Walt Whitman'"—so begins Mark Doty's essay "Insatiable." For readers who think of Whitman as "the good gray poet," the idea that he would be the model for a vampire is astonishing, and Doty is counting on that reaction.

Often, as you research your topic, you will come across a sentence or two that immediately triggers an "aha moment": yes, you'll think, that's exactly what I want to talk about. Rather than burying the quotation deep in your essay, why not share it right away with your readers so that they, too, can be inspired?

Use an "If ... Then ..." Statement

Verlyn Klinkenborg's essay on light pollution, "Our Vanishing Night," commences with a familiar grammatical structure: "If humans were truly at home under the light of the moon and stars, we would go in darkness happily, the midnight world as visible to us as it is to the vast number of nocturnal species on this planet."

As this example demonstrates, in an "if ... then ..." statement, the word "then" is often implied rather than stated in the second half of the sentence. This type of structure is called a "conditional sentence": the opening clause expresses the condition, and the main clause states the consequence of that condition. Klinkenborg uses the construction to express how things are *not*, rather than how they are, a strategy writers often use. Because we don't "go in darkness happily," she suggests, we must not be "truly at home under the light of the moon and stars."

Use a Simile or Metaphor

Jerald Walker starts his family memoir "The Mechanics of Being" with a simile: "A decade after dropping out of high school, I'd managed to arrive, like some survivor of a tragedy at sea, on the shores of a community college."

A **simile**, you may remember, is a comparison between two unlike things using "like" or "as." In the example above, the author is like a shipwrecked sailor, and the community college is like the shore on which he has finally washed up. A **metaphor** is a direct comparison between two unlike things: "I am a shipwrecked sailor washed up on the shores of a community college."

Similes and metaphors are called **figurative language**—non-literal language that alters or exaggerates the usual meanings of words. We associate the use of figurative language with poetry, and if you want to give your opening the power of a good poem, similes and metaphors can work wonders.

While I've focused on first sentences in the above examples, you may well need two or three or four sentences to accomplish the task of hooking your reader into your essay. That's fine. Here, for instance, is the opening to another *Best American Essay*, Gregory Orr's "Return to Hayneville," which clearly depends on the second sentence for its impact: "I was born and raised in rural upstate New York, but who I am began with a younger brother's death in a hunting accident when I was twelve and he was eight. I held the gun that killed him."

There are, of course, many more possible types of openings than those listed above, and you can mix and match the ones I've described. You might use a simile as part of an intriguing question, or exaggerate for comic effect in a list, or forward a claim that you intend to disprove in a surprising declarative sentence. What's important is that you attend to your opening sentences with the same care you gave to your thesis statement.

Using the models above, let's imagine several striking beginnings for the essay proposed in Chapter 4 on the legalization of marijuana.

An essay on legalization might open with an intriguing question:

If you accidently tumbled into someone at a party—someone big and potentially bad—which person would you rather face: a young man who had just smoked a bowl of Mango Kush, or a guy who had polished off a pint of whiskey?

That's kind of funny, but it could be risky in a conservative environment. Will your instructor think you are out partying all the time rather than doing your schoolwork? Maybe an allusion to an outmoded belief, with a touch of comic exaggeration, might work better:

Picture, if you will, the stereotypical pot smoker: twenty-something, red-eyed, unwashed, lounging on a friend's couch, staring glassy-eyed at cartoons while munching from a bag of barbecue-flavored potato chips, a half-smoked joint pinched between his thumb and fingertips.

That's clever, but where is it going? If this is the stereotypical stoner, what might someone else who smokes pot look like? You might continue from the previous sentence with some storytelling, as follows:

Now picture this instead: Eloise, an eighty-five-year-old grandmother sitting in her living room. On the walls are pictures of her children and grandchildren. From the kitchen comes the smell of apple pie baking in the oven. She is dying of cancer: she holds a half-smoked joint between her thumb and fingertips.

While it's enjoyable as a writer to create these mini-scenes, if you think back to our Chapter 4 thesis statement, you'll recall that it has four main points. Legalizing marijuana will save money by 1) eliminating the need for costly enforcement of marijuana laws, and 2) reducing the amount of money spent on building and maintaining prisons because there will be fewer inmates. The thesis also argues that legalization will collect revenue for the government through 3) sales tax on marijuana and 4) income taxes on workers in the marijuana industry.

As vivid as the opening sentences about the stoner dude and Grandma Eloise may be, they don't connect especially well to the thesis. We need to focus on financial issues instead:

> How much money would our government make if marijuana were legalized?

This is an intriguing question, one that should lead us quickly and surely to our thesis.

As with all writing, the first thing you think of may not be the best. If you're having a hard time composing a catchy opening and none of these suggestions inspires you, you can always open up a book of essays and see what other writers have done.

🚫 **Avoid This Common Error: "In today's society...."** Unable to think of any other way to begin their essays, students often use the first thing that pops into their heads. One of the most common fallback openings is "In today's society." Not only is this a cliché of academic writing—one that is guaranteed to make your instructor cringe—it is entirely unnecessary. Unless you indicate differently, your reader will always automatically assume you are talking about "today's society."

TOPIC OVERVIEW

Picture this: You're in your room in front of your computer. You've just finished writing an opening sentence you're quite proud of, but now it's time to begin writing the topic overview leading to your thesis statement. *Why bother spending much time on this?* you think. *My instructor knows the topic far better than I do, and is obviously already fascinated by it.* You may find this surprising, but that may not be the case. In a first-year writing class, where instructors often assign essays on subjects outside of their expertise, your professor may be only marginally more familiar with the topic than you are.

Instructors assign topics because they assume students will like them, or a colleague has recommended the topic, or a department chair has told all the instructors to cover certain material. Even if professors are enthusiastic and knowledgeable about their topics, they may have taught them so many times already that they secretly never want to read another paper on the subject.

It's a mistake, therefore, to assume that you can coast through your introduction. Instead, assume your instructor desperately needs you to ignite, or reignite, her or his interest in the topic.

Hopefully, you've begun doing that with a spectacular opening sentence (Point A). Hopefully, too, you will impress your professor with a smart, precise thesis statement (Point C). But how do you get from Point A to Point C?

The answer is to think of the middle of your introductory paragraph, the topic overview, as a bridge bringing your reader from your opening hook to the main focus of the essay. You don't want to clog the bridge up with traffic, as it were, but it never hurts to do some research that you might use later in your essay.

Our opening question, for instance, "How much money would our government make if marijuana were legalized?" could certainly use some concrete answers that can only be found through research. A look at the library database combined with a focused Internet search should, at this early stage in the drafting process, be enough to return some interesting information on the four main points to be covered in our essay.

With regard to saving money by eliminating the enforcement of marijuana laws, the website of the National Organization for the Reform of Marijuana Laws (NORML) claims that "Taxpayers annually spend between $7.5 billion and $10 billion arresting and prosecuting individuals for marijuana violations." That's a huge number, but the source—a group dedicated to legalizing marijuana—could be biased.

A bit more searching leads to an article in the liberal-leaning online news magazine *Huffington Post*, entitled "One Marijuana Arrest Occurs Every 42 Seconds in U.S.: FBI Report." Matt Ferner's piece notes that the FBI's Uniform Crime Reporting data indicates "there were a total of 1.5 million drug arrests made nationwide in 2011, and out of those arrests, about 750,000 were for marijuana (just under half, 49.5 percent)." The article goes on to quote Neill Franklin, a retired Baltimore police officer who heads a group called Law Enforcement Against Prohibition (LEAP). Franklin states, "Even excluding the costs involved for later trying and then imprisoning these people, taxpayers are spending between one and a half to three billion dollars a year just on the police and court time involved in making these arrests." That's significantly lower than the NORML figure of $7.5 to 10 billion, but it's probably better to err on the conservative side when writing about a controversial topic.

We're not doing the full research for our essay right now, so the *Huffington Post* pieces provide sufficient information for our first main point. A new search, for specifics on the costs of housing those convicted of marijuana crimes, returns "Pot Prisoners Cost Americans $1 Billion a Year," an article by Paul Armentano on the alternative news website AlterNet. Armentano cites a US Department of Justice report that shows "taxpayers are spending more than $1 billion annually to imprison pot offenders."

Again, we're building a bridge, not an entire city, so that $1 billion annually will allow us to move on to a search for the amount of revenue that would likely be generated through sales and income taxes. Our search leads to a **white paper**—that is, a government or business report on an important issue—called "The Budgetary Impact of Ending Drug Prohibition" by Jeffrey A. Miron and Katherine Waldock, published by the conservative Cato Institute, which states that "the legalization of marijuana would yield annual tax revenue in the United States of $8.7 billion."

That's more than enough research to build a bridge from the opening question to the thesis statement. In fact, in the process of arriving at a specific answer to our opening question, we've collected information that will be useful in the body paragraphs of the essay.

Still, there's something missing. The total of the experts' savings and revenue predictions equals $11 billion. That sounds like a huge sum, but just what would that amount of money buy? As a point of comparison, we should be looking for something that benefits many people, obviously. And why not focus on the most vulnerable among us: children. A little research reveals that the US Department of Agriculture spent $11.6 billion on the National School Lunch Program in 2012. Perfect. We're ready to write.

An introduction using our research might read as follows (the topic overview is in **bold**):

How much money would our government make if marijuana were legalized? **The answer, according to academic experts and the government itself, is at least 11 *billion* dollars. According to the United States Department of Agriculture, that's about the cost of the National School Lunch Program. In other words, the money wasted waging the losing war on marijuana could instead be spent ensuring that no child ever goes hungry at school. Yes, there are other solid motivations for repealing the prohibition on pot: forbidding people from using it clearly hasn't worked; the profits from illegal drugs end up in the hands of criminals; and marijuana is considerably less dangerous than alcohol, the *other* recreational**

drug. However, the most important reason to legitimize pot is financial. Legalization will eliminate the need for costly enforcement of marijuana laws and reduce the expense of building and maintaining prisons. Our government will not only save money, but will also earn revenue through sales tax on marijuana and income tax from the many citizens working in the marijuana industry.

A few things to remember about writing the topic overview:

- *Make a clear connection between the opening and the thesis.* Remember that we rejected several possible openings because they weren't relevant enough to our thesis.
- *Be succinct.* Don't rush, but don't linger over the middle of your introduction. Especially if you've written a strong opening, you don't want to lose momentum by getting tangled up in the details of your topic.
- *Revise your thesis as you draft.* Until you turn in your final draft, your thesis is always a "working thesis"—it is subject to change. Sometimes those changes may be substantial. Other times, as in the introduction above, the material preceding the thesis may only require you to change the wording.

ENDING WITH YOUR THESIS

The placement of the thesis at the end of the introductory paragraph will be second nature to many students, but especially if you are passionate about pushing boundaries, you may resent the idea that your introduction must always end with your thesis statement. After all, in the "creative nonfiction" being written in creative writing and journalism classes on other parts of campus, the thesis might not appear until the end of the essay, or in the late middle, or it might never be specifically stated at all, but only implied.

In an academic essay, however, ending your opening paragraph with your thesis serves two important functions:

- *It signals that you are aware of the conventions of academic writing.* Granted, there are disciplines, like creative writing and journalism, where innovative approaches to essay structure are rewarded. That may be the case in your class, too. But if it's not, or if you're unsure, better to err on the side of a more traditional approach.
- *It provides you and your professor with a clear roadmap of your essay.* Ending with your thesis is a smart way to ensure that you stay on track as you write. Moreover, a thesis statement at the end of the introduction is

especially helpful for instructors with heavy grading loads, as it allows them to quickly check and recheck how well you have supported your main arguments.

Timesaver Tip: If you can't generate a strong hook, begin writing the essay and return to the introduction later on. One of the great advantages of writing an out-of-class essay is that you don't have to do everything in sequence. You *will* want to have a working thesis when you start writing, but if you can't come up with those great opening sentences, or you haven't quite figured out how to bridge the opening and the thesis, go ahead and start writing the paper. As you write, ideas for crafting your introduction will come to you.

Questions and Suggestions FOR You

1. Try out several different opening sentences for your introduction. Be creative. Write the start of an essay that you yourself would want to read.
2. Do some research on your topic to help bridge the opening sentences and your thesis statement. Remember that while you don't want to go into great detail at this point, a specific example or two will show that you have been thinking seriously about your topic. And be sure to save any potentially useful research in a place where you can easily find it as you draft your body paragraphs.
3. Revise your thesis so that it more accurately reflects the contents of your introductory paragraph.

Questions and Suggestions FROM You

List three questions you still have after reading this section. Start by reviewing the chapter. If that method doesn't inspire three questions, think about the overall topic of introductions. What don't you know about writing introductory paragraphs that you would still like to know?

1. _____

_____

_____

_____

_____

2. _____

_____

_____

_____

_____

3. _____

_____

_____

_____

_____

Describe one activity related to writing introductory paragraphs *not mentioned in this chapter* that you think would be helpful to do in class. Any successful activity in any course you've ever taken might serve as a model.

_____

_____

_____

_____

_____

CHAPTER SEVEN

Body Paragraphs: And I Ought to Keep Reading Because?

PARAGRAPH STRUCTURE
TRANSITIONS
EXPERT OPINIONS AND CONCRETE EVIDENCE
QUOTATIONS
INTERVIEWS AND SURVEYS
NARRATIVE AND DESCRIPTION
MULTIMODAL MOVES

This chapter covers the hardest work of essay writing: crafting the body paragraphs—that is, the paragraphs between your introduction and conclusion—which make up the bulk of your essay. It's the longest chapter in the book, and it reflects where the majority of your writing time will be spent.

When students truly flounder, when they are ready to wave the white flag and surrender, it is usually at this stage in the writing process, when so much difficult thought is involved. Don't give up, though. The pages that follow include numerous concrete and specific suggestions for packing your body paragraphs with more than enough valuable material to satisfy even the most demanding instructor.

There's no denying that writing your body paragraphs can be challenging. But everything worthwhile is.

Jump in.

PARAGRAPH STRUCTURE

Most instructors reading academic essays will expect your body paragraphs to have four main components:

1. *A Topic Sentence*: The topic sentence refers back to a specific point in the thesis and announces the main idea that will be covered in the paragraph. Usually the topic sentence begins the paragraph, although sometimes, because of stylistic considerations, you might decide to make it your second sentence. Just as the thesis statement controls the content of the essay, the topic sentence dictates what is included in the paragraph.

2. *Supporting Evidence*: The topic sentence is a claim that needs proof to be believed, so the bulk of your body paragraph is composed of supporting evidence. As you read through this chapter, you'll be introduced to a variety of ways in which you can bolster that claim: quotations from experts, interviews, surveys, narratives and descriptions, charts and graphs, images and sounds. As you gather (and discard) material for your body paragraph, you'll want to ask yourself, 1) is my evidence persuasive?, and 2) is it directly relevant to my topic sentence?

3. *Analysis and Commentary*: Just as important as the evidence you produce to support your topic sentence is your analysis of that material. Your commentary should demonstrate why the evidence supports your topic sentence, which may include addressing potential counter-arguments: anticipating the likely opinion of an opponent of your point of view is generally a stronger tactic than ignoring it.

4. *A Concluding Sentence*: The concluding sentence or sentences should not simply repeat the topic sentence. Ideally, you've made forward progress in your essay, and the final sentence should sum up that progress *without announcing the topic of the next paragraph*. That's important: it can get very confusing for readers if you end each body paragraph with the topic sentence for the following paragraph.

So far, we've looked at possible ways of developing essays on the challenges of attending college for first-generation students, legalizing marijuana, and physician-assisted dying. Let's shift the focus in this chapter to another frequent topic in first-year writing classes—one that, unfortunately, rarely seems to be out of the news: gun control.

Each part of the paragraph below is labeled in the left margin, with triple bars (|||) inside the paragraph indicating where the topic sentence, evidence, analysis and commentary, and concluding sentence begin.

Topic Sentence However one feels about the possession of shotguns, pistols and rifles for hunting and sport shooting, there can be no doubt that semi- and fully automatic assault weapons cause far more harm than good and have no place in our society. ||| Think of the bloodshed in schools alone over a single five and a half year period. A *Mother Jones* article entitled "A Guide to Mass Shootings in America" lists, among many others, the following murderers who used military style *Evidence* weapons to commit their crimes: Seung-Hui Cho, who on April 16, 2007, killed 32 people and wounded 17 others at Virginia Tech; One Goh, who, on April 7, 2012, shot seven students and wounded three others at Oikos University in Oakland, California; and Adam Lanza, who on December 14, 2012, killed 20 first-graders, six teachers and staff members, and his own mother in Newtown, Connecticut. ||| The names of the companies who manufactured the weapons are familiar: Glock, Walther, Ruger. We know these names from movies and video games, and clearly America's *Analysis &* romance with guns played a role in these killings. *Commentary* Mental illness was also a factor in the cases listed above. However, we do live in a free country: we cannot control the media. And treatment for mental illness, especially for those who do not seek it, can seem like an insurmountable obstacle. Nevertheless, we can make a real and determined effort to get assault weapons out of the hands of those who would harm us. ||| *Refutation of* Granted, some law-abiding citizens do try to make a *Counter-* case for possessing assault weapons. According to a *argument* CNN report by Thom Patterson, among the reasons people own military-style rifles is because shooting them is a form of relaxation, "like playing golf"; they are "cool"; and the owners are "fascinated with the second amendment." However, none of these reasons comes close to justifying the access to assault weapons by someone like Seung-Hui Cho or Adam Lanza. ||| A reasonable response to gun control must begin with *Concluding* the immediate and systematic outlawing of semi- and *Sentence* fully automatic assault weapons.

As you can see, *logos* or reason dominates the traditional body paragraph. The initial claim made by the topic sentence is supported by plentiful specific and concrete evidence. The analysis of the evidence includes a refutation of a potential counterargument (military-style weapons aren't *all* bad) and ends with a concluding sentence that echoes, without simply repeating, the topic sentence. In short, a strong body paragraph in an academic essay is

- *Organized*: both reader and writer have a clear sense of why each element in the paragraph appears where it does;
- *Coherent*: it briefly repeats key words and phrases to remind readers of the paragraph's topic;
- *Supported by persuasive evidence*: without concrete, specific, and detailed evidence to back up your thesis statement, it won't matter how organized or coherent the paragraph is.

Timesaver Tip: Turn your topic sentence into a question, and then see if your paragraph answers it. One of the quickest and most reliable ways to make sure your paragraph supports your topic sentence is to turn your topic sentence into a question, and then decide whether or not that question is fully answered by the paragraph's evidence and analysis. In the paragraph above, for instance, we might rework the topic sentence as follows: "Do semi- and fully automatic assault weapons cause far more harm than good in our society?" Based on the information provided in the paragraph, the answer would seem to be a resounding "Yes."

TRANSITIONS

Reading can be hard work, and it always helps if you signal when you're moving from one idea or topic to the next. Make sure you use transition words and phrases to guide your reader along the path of your argument. The paragraph above, for instance, seems to be following a paragraph on hunting and sport shooting: "However one feels about the possession of shotguns, pistols and rifles for hunting and sport shooting...." The word "However" signifies a movement to a new topic, while the repetition of the previous topic, "the possession of shotguns, pistols and rifles for hunting and sport shooting," briefly reminds the reader of the material that has just been covered.

Transitions are most effective when they are part of topic sentences, but you should also use them in your body paragraph to indicate shifts in the direction of your essay. In the sample paragraph above, words like "however," "nevertheless," and "granted" act as signposts whenever the argument is about to take a turn.

Below is a list of transitions grouped by the type of shift they make as you move from paragraph to paragraph and sentence to sentence:

Addition/Emphasis
also
and
further
in addition
in fact
indeed
moreover

Cause and Effect
as a result
because
consequently
therefore

Comparison
also
in comparison
likewise
similarly
too

Concession
admittedly
certainly
granted
I concede that
of course

Contrast
although
but
by contrast
despite
however
nevertheless
nonetheless
on the contrary
still
while
yet

Examples
consider
for example
for instance
in particular
specifically
to illustrate

EXPERT OPINIONS AND CONCRETE EVIDENCE

"The reason I read nonfiction," essayist Phillip Lopate writes, "is to follow an interesting mind." Your instructor is likely to agree with that sentiment, and one of the best ways to demonstrate an interesting mind in an academic essay is to include a compelling mixture of expert opinion and concrete evidence in each paragraph, with emphasis on the evidence.

Expert Opinions

Drawing on the opinions of others is an essential component of academic writing. We look to experts to give their judgments about controversial issues, believing that their mastery of a field gives them special authority to speak on a topic.

But how do you judge whether or not someone is an authority? A true expert is likely to meet all three of these criteria. She or he

1. holds an advanced degree in the subject or has significant relevant professional experience;
2. has published books or articles in scholarly journals and/or national periodicals;
3. offers credible evidence to support her/his opinions.

Suppose you offer the following opinion: "Everyone should have the right to bear arms." What comes next? If you haven't done any research or invention on the topic, you're likely—in the absence of any real supporting evidence—to fall back on sweeping statements:

> Everyone should have the right to bear arms. It's a known fact that without guns this country would not be what it is today. History has shown time and again that when we are threatened by tyranny, men and women with full-on firepower have been there to protect everyone's liberty.

This is opinion of the least convincing sort. "Known fact," for instance, in addition to being a cliché, implicitly makes a claim that is never proven. *Who* knows the fact? What's the proof? Likewise, the general assertion "History has shown time and time again..." has no evidence to reinforce it. Men and women with "full-on firepower" may well have protected some people's liberty. But *"everyone's"*? And when? Where? Why? And *how*, for that matter?

Compare these vague abstractions with a quotation from a single expert in the field:

> Everyone should have the right to bear arms. As Georgetown University law professor Randy E. Barnett argues in "Was the Right to Keep and Bear Arms Conditioned on Service in an Organized Militia?," an article originally published in *The Scholarly Commons*, "we just may need the militia again one day, as we did on September 11th. When we do, it may well be under circumstances where it would be better if its members have access to their own weapons to arm themselves."

Granted, Barnett's argument is based primarily on his own interpretation of the Second Amendment, but the fact that he is a professor at a highly respected law school, and that he alludes to a specific historical event as a possible precedent, gives his opinion far more weight than if it were offered by someone without any specialized training in constitutional law—a gun-owning friend of a friend, say, or a member of the cast of *Duck Dynasty*.

Avoid This Common Error: Citing the opinion of non-experts. Don't cite the opinion of someone who isn't especially qualified to speak on your topic. An essay by another undergraduate student posted online may well make some valid points, but wouldn't it be much more persuasive to cite that student's professor, or the sources the student cites? Yes, some experts write blogs, which can make for perfectly acceptable evidence. But many more *non*-experts write blogs. In an academic essay, those non-expert opinions don't count for much.

Concrete Evidence

In academic writing, the most persuasive opinions are generally supported by concrete evidence. Let's move to the other side of the gun-control debate for a moment with another broad statement that badly needs evidence to support it: "Opposition to gun control is racist."

A search through the library database reveals several scholarly articles based on surveys, interviews, and **literature review** (an examination of the scholarship to date) that do, indeed, support this contention. Let's add one such piece of evidence to the initial claim:

Opposition to gun control is racist, and there is statistical evidence to prove it. "Racism, Gun Ownership and Gun Control," a 2013 article published in the *Public Library of Science* by four British and Australian professors, is based on an exhaustive survey with tightly controlled variables. The authors conclude: "Attitudes towards guns in many US whites appear to be influenced, like other policy preferences, by illogical racial biases."

That's fairly persuasive, especially if we begin examing the statistical evidence that supports their claim. Adding yet another scholarly source doubles the force of the argument:

"Race, Fear, and Firearms" reviews decades' worth of studies on the subject. The article, which was published in the March 2009 edition of the *Journal of African American Studies* maintains:

A causal examination of the history of gun control laws in the U.S. would leave most readers with the inescapable conclusion that a sizable number of these laws at the federal, state, and local levels have been motivated by racism and xenophobia.... The pattern is clear. If there is a "dangerous" population one wishes to control, demonize that population: they are agitators, malcontents, degenerates, criminals. (69–70)

In short, every piece of evidence you can offer to support the opinion forwarded by your thesis is a sound investment of your research and writing time.

QUOTATIONS

In Chapter 2, we discussed the difference between summary, paraphrase, and quotation. You'll recall that a **summary** is a concise statement of the main points found in a piece of writing. To **paraphrase** is to rephrase in your own words something said or written by someone else. And a **quotation** reflects the *exact words* of the writer or speaker, including capitalization and punctuation.

The opinions and evidence you use to support your thesis statement will come in all three forms. You'll use summary when you need to boil down an extended argument into a sentence or two. You'll employ paraphrase when you want to cite an author's idea but you think you can do it more clearly in your own words. In general, though, a properly introduced direct quotation is the strongest form of evidence in an academic essay. Even providing a few words of quotation from each of your main sources shows not only that you understood the source, but also that you were able to find a perfect moment in the article or book where you and the writer were exactly in synch.

Additionally, a quotation offers some proof that you have actually *read* the work to which you are referring. Professors are rightly suspicious of essays that feature a long list of end citations but few or no specific quotations in the body of the essay. Papers like these suggest a student author has skimmed quickly over the titles of books and articles but has never taken the trouble to look at the works themselves.

Signal Phrases

In academic essays, a signal phrase (or sentence) introduces a quotation, summary, or paraphrase. A full signal phrase includes

- the title of the work being cited,
- the author's name,
- the author's professional title, which establishes her/his authority.

Here's an example of a signal phrase leading into a direct quotation:

> In their book *The Gun Debate: What Everyone Needs to Know*, Duke University public policy professors Philip J. Cook and Kristin A. Goss point out that "Mass shootings are traumatic for victims, for their loved ones, and for communities, even nations, whose collective sense of security they shake" (46).

Of course, including all this information in every single signal phrase isn't always necessary. However, it's better to err on the side of including too much information rather than too little.

Citing Your Sources Internally Using MLA

At the end of the above quotation, the page number from which the quotation was taken is

- listed in parentheses,
- on the outside of the quotation marks,
- but inside the period.

Here are three more tips on using the sometimes complicated rules of Modern Language Association documentation to quote from a work:

- Let's say *The Gun Debate* is a website instead of a book. If you introduced the quotation as above, with both the title and the authors, you would not need a parenthetical citation at the end of the sentence because websites have no page numbers.
- If, however, no specific information about the source was provided in the signal phrase, you would end the quotation with the authors' last names: (Cook and Goss 46). This would direct the reader to the source listed in the references at the end of the paper.
- If the title of the website was listed, but there were no authors, your citation would read: (*Gun Debate*). Of course, if there were no authors listed on a website, you probably wouldn't trust it, so you wouldn't be citing it in the first place.

These are just the very basics, of course. For a list of the most common MLA citations, see Appendix II.

Ellipsis

You'll notice that the first sentence in the quotation above from "Race, Fear, and Firearms" ends with an **ellipsis**, a series of three spaced dots indicating some words have been omitted. Use an ellipsis (plural: ellipses) when parts of the quotation are irrelevant to your essay. For example, you might say: "Mass shootings are traumatic for victims ... and for communities, even nations, whose collective sense of security they shake" (46).

However, according to Mignon Fogarty, the editor and author also known as "Grammar Girl," "most style guides don't call for an ellipsis when you omit something at the end of a quote," and using "an ellipsis at the beginning of a quote is also not usually necessary." You can de-clutter your writing a bit by leaving out the ellipsis when you cut off the start or finish of a quotation.

A less honorable use of ellipses is to remove the parts of your quotation that don't support your claim. You see this often in movie studios' use of film reviews, when a few words of praise are excerpted from a long passage of criticism. In academic essays, however, you should not "cherry pick" short quotations from a source that generally disagrees with you. If you do quote from a hostile source, make sure to acknowledge that you and your source are mostly at odds on the topic. For instance:

> While professors Smith and Wesson largely ignore the horrendous effects of gun violence, they do admit that "gun safety is an integral part of gun ownership."

A Quotation within a Quotation

When you quote a writer who is quoting someone else, you need to indicate that you have a quotation within a quotation. You do this by placing double quotation marks on the outside ("), then single quotation marks (') inside the quotation to indicate where that second quotation begins and ends:

> In "The Reckoning," a *New Yorker* profile of Adam Lanza's father, Peter, Andrew Solomon notes that Peter "constantly thinks about what he could have done differently and wishes he had pushed harder to see Adam. 'Any variation on what I did and how my relationship was had to be good, because no outcome could be worse.'"

Modifying a Quotation with Brackets

Sometimes the grammar of your quotation may not fit the context in which it appears, or the identity of the persons mentioned in the quotation may not be clear. In these cases, you may need to add a word or two in brackets [ ] to indicate that you have made a slight change for clarity's sake.

Say, for example, you are writing an essay on the National Rifle Association. One of your sources continually alludes to executive vice-president Wayne LaPierre as "he" or "him" rather than using his name. You might use brackets as follows: "When a group of NRA members are gathered in a room and the talk turns to [Wayne LaPierre], there is often a respectful silence followed by a sudden eruption of applause."

[sic]

As noted above, a direct quotation requires that you use the writer's or speaker's exact words. Not every quotation is grammatically perfect, of course, so when you want to indicate that a mistake was made by your source rather than by you, insert the Latin phrase *sic* (which means "so" or "thus") in brackets right after the error. For example: "Smith and Wesson claim in a recent article, 'The world are [*sic*] full of gun control fanatics.'"

Titles of Shorter and Longer Works

The titles of shorter works go inside quotation marks, while longer works are italicized. For instance, the article "Race, Fear, and Firearms" is in quotation marks; the journal in which the article appears, *Journal of African American Studies*, is italicized. Books are also italicized: *The Gun Debate: What Everyone Needs to Know.*

You'll notice, too, that the first and the main words in each title are capitalized, while less important words are not: "Race," "Fear," "Firearms," but not "and." Similarly: *The Gun Debate: What Everyone Needs to Know.*

Sentence-Length Quotations

When you write a sentence of introduction for a sentence or more of quotation, introduce the quotation with a colon, like this: "Sentence-length quotations preceded by a sentence of introduction should be introduced with a colon."

Block Quotations

Quotations of more than four lines should be indented in a block quotation. You can see this in our quotation from "Race, Fear, and Firearms" above. The basic rules for a block quotation are as follows:

> Indent 5 spaces, or one tab. A block quotation is usually introduced by a sentence ending with a colon. You don't use quotation marks, as the indentation signals to your reader that everything in the block quotation is a direct quotation. If you are using MLA documentation, when you come to the end of the quotation, cite the page number—if there is one—or the names of the author(s) in parentheses on the *outside* of the period. (46)

Remember, the longer the quotation, the more responsibility you have for discussing it in your article. A long quotation dropped into a paragraph without any analysis or explanation of the quotation's relevance to your argument looks like what it probably is: a blatant attempt to run up the essay's word count.

Signal Phrase, Quotation, Comment

In their excellent book *They Say / I Say*, Gerald Graff and Cathy Birkenstein popularized the phrase "quotation sandwich" to describe a technique professors have long recommended for properly introducing a quotation into an academic essay. A quotation sandwich 1) establishes the authority of the author of your quotation and indicates where you found it, 2) provides a quotation from that source, and 3) directly applies the quotation to your larger topic.

Here's the basic structure of a quotation sandwich—signal phrase, quotation, comment about the quotation—with each section highlighted by a different font:

Introduce the author and the place where the material originally appeared. [BREAD]

THE QUOTATION. [MEAT]

Directly apply the quotation to your topic. [BREAD]

And here's an example of a quotation sandwich for an essay on gun control, with the appropriate sections highlighted:

In their book *The Gun Debate: What Everyone Needs to Know*, Duke University Public Policy professors Philip J. Cook and Kristin A. Goss point out that "Mass shootings are traumatic for victims, for their loved ones, and for communities, even nations, whose collective sense of security they shake" (46). **Cook and Goss are right to note how far the shock and suffering radiate from the actual victims. It is this unnecessary and widespread trauma that leads advocates of gun control to argue so strongly for the immediate and total ban of all automatic weapons.**

Synonyms for "Says" and "Writes"

When quoting sources, you will often fall into the pattern of writing "Professor A. says…," or "Dr. Z. writes…." While it's usually better to err on the side of bland—"She writes…" is better than "She expostulates…"—you will want to vary the "verbs of attribution" to keep your writing from becoming boring. Here are a few of the most common synonyms:

acknowledges	maintains
adds	notes
admits	observes
affirms	points out
argues	proposes
believes	reveals
claims	shows
concedes	speculates
concludes	states
emphasizes	suggests
explains	thinks
implies	warns
indicates	wonders
insists	worries

Avoid This Common Error: "He quoted…." To quote someone is to repeat her or his words. Therefore, when a source is speaking, you would not say, "Professor A. quoted, 'Our research suggests dire consequences for the country.'" Professor A. is not quoting anyone: she is stating the results of her research. If Professor A. wants to quote Dr. Z., that's fine, of course, but be careful how you use the words "quote" and "quoted."

INTERVIEWS AND SURVEYS

Interviews

When experts on a topic write articles, they tend to use their professional, scholarly voice. That tone can certainly be persuasive, but sometimes it's also quite dry. One way to find more "quotable quotes" from experts is to look for published interviews. If, during your research, the names of the same few experts keep coming up, try your search with one of the experts' names and the word "interview"—you'll be pleased by how often you find the person speaking in terms that are much easier to understand.

Of course, you won't always find a published interview on your topic, and the interviewer doesn't always ask the questions you might have. Conducting your own interview not only gives you control over the questions asked to an expert, but also demonstrates considerable individual initiative. Your instructor will be impressed that you took the time to augment your more traditional research with a personal Q & A.

Whether the person you are interviewing is a professor on campus, a professional in the community, or someone you contact via the Internet, *be respectful of the person's time.* Remember that an expert who agrees to an interview with a student has nothing to gain: she or he is doing you a favor, so act accordingly.

You will save your own time and your interviewee's by adhering to the following suggestions:

- Make sure you write out a list of questions before you conduct your interview.
- At the same time, be open to leaving your set questions and following up on interesting comments made by your subject.
- Focus on the person's expertise—don't get sidetracked talking about issues that are irrelevant to your interview.
- Take notes and use a digital recorder (with the interviewee's permission) if the interview is in person or on the telephone. Note: While an email interview doesn't have the same spontaneity as one conducted in person, over the phone, or via Skype, it does have the advantage of already being written out for you when you are composing your essay.
- Ask the interviewee if they want to add anything else before you close.

Good interview questions tend to be a combination of specific and open-ended questions. Imagine, for instance, the sorts of questions you might ask the head of your campus security about gun control:

Specific

- How many security guards are on campus at any one time?
- How, minute-by-minute, would our campus respond to a school shooting?
- What, specifically, would be the role of campus security?
- Do you know of any threats that have been made to students, staff, or faculty?

General

- What are your biggest fears as the head of campus security?
- What goes through your mind when you hear about the latest shooting on another campus?
- What, if anything, can our country do about school shootings?

Ideally, both types of questions would reward you with valuable information for your essay. The head of security's response to the specific questions about the number of security guards on campus would be a quick fact that you could drop into your paper: "Chief Suarez notes that there are always at least three security guards on campus, day or night." Similarly, his description of the campus's plan for a school shooting would provide a wealth of detail about how prepared, or unprepared, your campus is for a tragedy.

Granted, more general questions can be hit or miss. The answer to the question about what goes through the chief's head after he hears about a school shooting elsewhere could be as simple as, "I just feel bad for everyone." Or he might launch into a surprising answer about how he can imagine the students on your campus feeling personally victimized by a shooting, and how passionately he feels about preventing that from happening. Even if most of the answers to a set of general questions are less than revelatory, the possibility that you might receive one remarkable answer makes them worth asking.

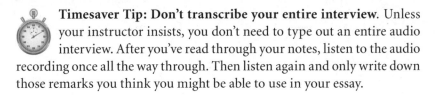 **Timesaver Tip: Don't transcribe your entire interview.** Unless your instructor insists, you don't need to type out an entire audio interview. After you've read through your notes, listen to the audio recording once all the way through. Then listen again and only write down those remarks you think you might be able to use in your essay.

Surveys

As with interviews, published surveys may give a broad and thorough response to the questions you are asking about your topic. Indeed, detailed professional surveys often form the backbone of scholarly articles. However, such studies may not reveal the sort of information you are looking for, and, as with interviews, conducting your own survey allows you to focus the questions and demonstrates dedication to your research that your professor will appreciate.

Obviously, the sort of survey you are likely to conduct will have a much smaller sample than one conducted by professionals and will probably draw on your classmates as respondents. As with interview questions, your survey questions will likely be of two types: direct and open-ended.

Direct questions on gun control might look like this:

Do you own a gun? Yes / No
Does anyone in your family own a gun? Yes / No
Do you think all automatic weapons should be banned? Yes / No

Collecting data from yes or no questions simply involves counting the number of surveys and calculating the percentage. If your class contains 28 students, and 10 of them own guns, then 36% of your classmates own guns ($10 \div 28 = .36$). Straightforward tabulation is particularly useful when a survey has a large population; however, small samplings, like those found in a single class, are limited in what they can tell you.

Probably more useful for an academic essay is what's called a "scaled response," a question or statement offering a range of responses. This takes longer to tabulate, but it allows for a more nuanced reply to your questions. Here are two scaled response questions:

Guns are necessary for individuals to protect themselves against government tyranny.
☐ Strongly agree
☐ Agree
☐ Neither agree nor disagree
☐ Disagree
☐ Strongly disagree

All automatic weapons should be banned.
☐ Strongly agree
☐ Agree
☐ Neither agree nor disagree
☐ Disagree
☐ Strongly disagree

Small direct and scaled response surveys can give you an interesting overview of your peers' views on a topic. However, if the primary purpose of your survey is to gather insights and possible quotations for your essay, you will also need to include open-ended questions like these:

Why is the gun lobby so strong?
What do you think is the single best method of reducing gun violence?

Don't, however, make your questions *too* open-ended. "How do you feel about gun control?" is likely to get you responses such as, "I don't like it" or "I think it's a good idea." A more directed question like those above should yield stronger results.

Unfortunately, as anyone who has ever tried to administer a survey knows, the toughest part is getting people to respond. You can use online applications like SurveyMonkey, but if the survey subjects are busy people like your classmates, you're much more likely to get a high rate of return if your instructor allows you a few minutes to conduct a short survey during class time.

NARRATIVE AND DESCRIPTION

So far, we've been focusing on relatively traditional academic writing. The material gathered from the methods described above could easily fit into the time-honored formula described at the beginning of this chapter: topic sentence + supporting evidence = solid body paragraph. Some instructors will warn you from straying too far from this accepted path.

Others, however, will be open to experimentation. One of the core principles of *Academic Writing Now* is that specific, concrete, and detailed examples are among the most persuasive forms of evidence. If you want readers to adopt your point of view, you need to show them why they should. That can mean turning to narrative and description, two hallmarks of creative or literary nonfiction. Taking this route means rethinking the structure of your body paragraph. While traditional topic sentences are not necessarily absent from creative nonfiction, paragraphs focusing on narrative and description generally have much more freedom to imply a topic rather than to state it outright.

Let's say you want to suggest how gun violence can sway a community in favor of tighter restrictions on gun ownership. Imagine you are at that point early in a body paragraph when you feel the need for a specific example, so you allude to the 2012 tragedy at Sandy Hook Elementary School in Newtown, Connecticut, as follows:

Many people who visited the Newtown memorials to the twenty slain children and six school personnel came away vowing never to allow another such tragedy.

This sentence is grammatically correct. It includes several solid pieces of information, including the number of victims and the fact that—as television coverage demonstrated—visitors to the Newtown memorials were often visibly moved and spoke out against gun violence. Nevertheless, the sentence doesn't allow us to actually *see* the memorial and the mourners. It's like looking at a Google map from satellite view rather than zooming down to street-level.

If you want something more vivid to draw your readers in, an online image search quickly reveals a number of photographs of the memorials posted by reliable news organizations. Your search could also lead to brief videos posted on CNN.com, visuals that will help you craft a mini-scene that shows your position without having to engage in name-calling. After taking notes on the photographs and videos, you might plunge in as follows:

> On a hillside covered with fallen leaves, twenty hand-painted wooden angels were staked into the wet ground. Votive candles flickered in the twilight, as the many bouquets of flowers withered in the cold. Dozens of stuffed animals crowded the scene, but the six-year-old victims of an unspeakable crime would never hold these teddy bears. A mentally ill young man may have pulled the trigger, but ultimately guns are to blame: it's no wonder so many people who visited the Newtown memorials shortly after the shooting at Sandy Hook Elementary School have joined the grieving parents in an effort to "truly honor the lives lost by turning . . . tragedy into a moment of transformation" (Sandy Hook Promise).

Creative writers know that visual imagery is crucial to bringing a scene to life, and the paragraph above draws heavily on the sense of sight. It doesn't matter that you weren't there. Your word picture is based on trustworthy evidence and makes good use of visual literacy, which we will discuss in the next section. Of course, print journalists published a number of moving accounts of the aftermath of the shooting, and in another essay you might well have drawn on someone else's descriptions rather than your own impressions. The important difference between the single sentence and the fully fleshed-out paragraph is how much richer and more *persuasive* the second passage is than the first.

Now let's suppose you are on the other side of the fence, wanting to write in favor of gun owners' rights. Imagine you are beginning to craft a paragraph and need some evidence to support your position. An online news search alerts you to a home invasion that occurred in Georgia a few weeks after the shootings in Connecticut. You write:

In January of 2013, Melinda Herman shot a man who broke into her home, "striking him five times" (Banks and Kiggins). If not for the fact that she was armed and trained to use her weapon, things might have gone very badly for Melinda and her two children.

Again, these two sentences are grammatically and factually correct. There's even a quotation from a short online article entitled "Homeowner Shoots Intruder in Walton County." The evidence presented does give some weight to the idea that in certain circumstances owning a gun could prove lifesaving, and if you were satisfied with a relatively bland account of the incident, you might move on.

However, while this was surely a dramatic and traumatic event, there's not much evidence of Ms. Herman's fear and distress in your writing. Using source material to recreate the scene would surely be more persuasive:

It was a chilly January morning in Walton County, east of Atlanta. Vacant lots and stands of pine separate the houses of the relatively new development of Henderson Ridge, so when Melinda Herman heard a splintering sound at her front door, she immediately gathered her 9-year old twins from the basement and hurried them up to a crawlspace in the attic.

Unfortunately for Melinda, the intruder, a recently released convict named Paul Slater, "wouldn't back down" (Banks and Kiggins). Local reporter Adam Murphy said that Slater used a crowbar "to open three doors as he chased Melinda Herman and her two children" through the house. Trapped in a dark corner and fearing for her life and the lives of her children, Melinda did what anyone would do: she fought back. She shot Slater five times, forcing him to flee the home. Not long afterwards, he crashed his car and was captured by police.

Melinda's husband, Donnie, was clearly moved by his wife's courage. Talking to television reporters, Donnie, a burly, bearded man who looks as though he is not given to excessive emotion, spoke haltingly, calling his wife "a hero. She protected her kids. She did what she was supposed to do as a responsible, prepared gun owner" (cbsatlanta.com).

It's a grim fact, but without a gun, chances are Melinda and her two children would be dead.

Naturally, your reader will assume you were nowhere near Walton County when all this took place, but, again, that doesn't mean you couldn't have legitimately gathered the material on your own. In the first place, you cite three sources, which demonstrates you've done some research. Your inquiry might have begun with a glance at a map of northern Georgia; it's easy to see that Walton County is in Atlanta's "exurbs," beyond the eastern suburbs. Aerial news videos of the house after the crime showed empty lots on all sides. The winter grass was brown, and a quick check of accuweather.com indicates the high temperature in Atlanta on the day of the crime was 51 degrees. The remainder of the information comes from reading the online article and watching two rebroadcasts of news segments posted online, the same segments that showed numerous views of the Hermans' home and the interview with Donnie. Yes, it took an extra fifteen minutes to get this information, but it was essentially "lightning research," and it makes all the difference between a few perfunctory sentences and a memorable bit of creative academic writing.

Another advantage of descriptive narrative writing is how portable it is throughout an essay. A passage like the one about Melinda Herman might work well in the heart of an essay, although it could just as easily serve as an introduction or a conclusion. And you can expand and contract description and narration to fit the purposes of individual paragraphs. Sometimes a paragraph that's heavy with facts and statistics can be made more readable with a brief anecdote, a sentence or two that richly evokes the world you are discussing. Other times, as in the paragraphs above, you may lean heavily on storytelling, with the research more in the background.

Granted, providing evidence for the claims you make in your essays is a crucial aspect of academic writing, as is focusing on your readers and your assignment. However, none of these basic requirements precludes you from writing essays that will matter to your readers because they matter to you. Given the choice of reading the flat, merely factual prose of the first examples versus the vivid narrative revisions, who wouldn't choose the latter? In the words of author Alice McDermott: "detail is good, precise detail is better, precise detail with many layers of meaning that contributes to the harmony and shape of the whole work is better still." McDermott is talking about fiction writing, but her comments also apply to good nonfiction writing.

Before you plunge fully into the world of narrative and description, first gauge your instructor's opinion on how appropriate those techniques are for an academic essay. However, even if your professor prefers a more conservative approach, a touch of storytelling here and a bit of description there can still go a long way toward making your essays worth savoring.

 Timesaver Tip: Take a break. It may seem counterintuitive when you're writing against a deadline, but sometimes a short, 10–20 minute break can give you the energy you need to return to your writing with renewed vigor and attention. Try a change of scenery, exercising, drinking a glass of water or tea, even taking a 10–15 minute "power nap" (but don't forget to set your alarm!).

MULTIMODAL MOVES

John R. MacArthur, the publisher of *Harper's Magazine*, points to "academic research showing that readers better comprehend sentences printed on paper than sentences constructed with pixels on screen." Nevertheless, MacArthur acknowledges he is in the minority in what he calls the age of "digital correctness."

Even as the average writing classroom remains devoted to the creation of "alphabetic text," many writing theorists are advocating for the use of multimodal technologies, which can mean anything from a combination of print and image, to a full digital essay driven by video and sound.

Your instructor will set the guidelines for your particular class, but whether or not your current professor advocates making multimodal moves, you may well be required to employ them in other classes. It's always good to consider your options.

Images

You'll notice how quickly an image gets your attention in a book like this one, which is composed mostly of text. A moment after taking in what you see below—an elderly woman wearing glasses and a bathrobe, standing in front of a window covered with lace curtains, a flashlight in one hand and a pistol in the other—your eyes probably move down to the caption, which reads, "An Elderly Woman Confronts a Home Invader."

An Elderly Woman Confronts a Home Invader

Even though many of us have used Photoshop and other image-altering software, photographs—as opposed to drawings or paintings—still carry the weight of the *real*. Suppose this photo was included in the middle of an essay opposing gun control. Seeing a poor woman defending herself and her home in the middle of the night, how could we *not* be on the side of gun ownership?

Upon further reflection, though we surely realize that, unless the intruder took this photograph, the scene is staged. In fact, the photo was purchased from Shutterstock, a company that specializes in selling generic images to businesses. Moreover, the caption itself is invented, with the phrase "Home *Invader*" chosen over the less menacing word "*Intruder.*"

What this means for you as someone composing an academic essay is two-fold. On the one hand, you recognize the power an image can have in persuading someone who is reading your essay. On the other hand, you must acknowledge how deceptive images can be. It is a difficult balancing act: wanting to sway your readers with a riveting image, while at the same time maintaining a sense of academic honesty and integrity. Clearly, there is no single "correct" way to introduce an image into your essay, but each time you do so, it's worth considering the implications of using a picture rather than words.

Let's jump back to the other side of the issue for a moment. Certainly, if we were arguing in favor of gun control, we could login to Shutterstock and purchase any number of photographs of intimidating men with guns. However, a more subtle, and potentially more powerful, approach would be to return to that sorrowful hill in Newtown, Connecticut, the one described in the previous section, with wooden angels representing the dead at the Sandy Hook Elementary School shooting.

Wooden Angels in a Yard Near Sandy Hook, December 16, 2012

Once more, we are drawing on our reader's sympathies—whether fairly or unfairly, it's hard to say. This photograph works primarily on the level of *pathos* (emotion) rather than *logos* (reason) or *ethos* (the speaker's credibility).

As you decide what, if any, images you want to choose and how you will arrange them, ask yourself the following questions:

- What is my overall goal for this essay?
- Which image(s) will best help me to accomplish that purpose?
- Where do I place the image(s)?
- How much writing, if any, do I need to properly contextualize the image(s)?
- How is my target audience likely to respond to my image(s)?
- How manipulative do I want to be?

That last question isn't meant to be flippant. Because images can be so powerful, writers sometimes feel that dropping one into an essay allows us to circumvent the more rigorous requirements of explanation and analysis. Yet an experienced reader/viewer like your instructor may well resent feeling as though he or she has been the victim of a clever visual trick.

On a more practical level, remember that as you choose images, you will need to acknowledge their original source in the same way you would if you were quoting a written source. And, even more importantly, you'll want to justify inclusion of the image with substantial written commentary. If you were using the photo of the wooden angels near Sandy Hook Elementary School, your commentary might take the form of a detailed narrative description, like the one in the section above, or it might take a more analytical form, like this:

The homeowner who decided to stake a flock of wooden angels into his yard clearly had his heart in the right place: he wanted to memorialize the victims of Adam Lanza's crazed shooting at a nearby elementary school on December 14, 2012. Stuffed animals have been placed at the foot of each angel, but there is something woefully incomplete about the scene. Yes, the gesture is all kindness, but one wonders if these small memorials of wood and paint, plush fur and stuffing might somehow dull the righteous anger of those in favor of gun control. Does this front yard display make us sad and sentimental rather than energized and activist?

Charts and Graphs

A business report without charts and graphs would seem practically useless in most corporations, yet academic essays tend to use them far less frequently. Not every academic essay will benefit from these visuals, but if you want to succinctly and forcefully convey statistical information, charts and graphs are worth considering.

One of the easiest charts to use is the pie chart, which shows how a whole is divided into several parts. As an example, let's return to our survey on gun ownership in class. You'll recall that of 28 students, 10 of them (or 36 per cent) owned guns. A pie chart showing that statistic would look like this:

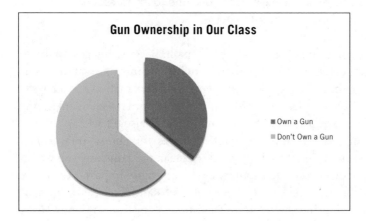

And here is a 3-D bar graph showing the responses to one of the survey questions above:

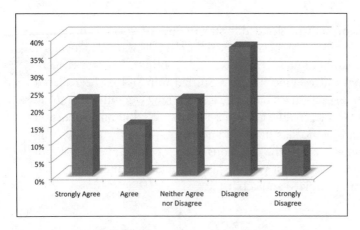

Class responses to the statement, "Guns are necessary for individuals to protect themselves against government tyranny"

Both the pie chart and the bar graph help readers visualize numerical data. However, the data from our imaginary class surveys is relatively even, although clearly there is a bias toward gun control. The pie chart would work best if our readers assumed that in our classroom either no one, or practically everyone, owned a gun. Similarly, the 3-D bar graph would be most effective in indicating students' wide range of opinions on gun control.

Charts and graphs tend to make the biggest impression when there is a striking disparity between data. Imagine, for instance, if the class survey had skewed strongly in favor of gun control. The chart above would now look like this:

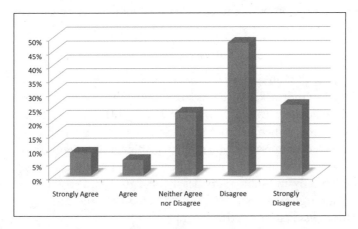

Typically in an academic essay, charts and graphs either generate discussion or are the visual culmination of an argument. In either case, remember that simply dropping a chart or graph in your essay isn't enough. You need to contextualize it for readers, making sure you explain why it appears and analyzing its implications for your overall argument.

Video

In a truly multimodal class, you might write your essay as a script and read it as a voice-over, so that the person viewing your essay only *hears* your text while watching the visuals you have selected to play on top of your narration. Such an essay would involve **storyboarding**—that is, making a sequence of images that represent the main goals of your essay—as well as a number of technical decisions we don't have room to cover here. Check with your instructor, though. If you are technically savvy, he or she may welcome the opportunity to see how an inventive student approaches a video version of the academic essay.

In a digital essay that focuses on alphabetic text, you would use video more selectively. You might, for instance, video an interview you conducted, and then place it strategically in the text so that your reader could actually see and hear what your interviewee had to say. Of course, you can download video clips from the Internet in the same way you might use a still image, but, again, you will need to cite the original source just as you would a print source.

Some questions to ask as you consider using videos in a digital essay:

- Is the video too long?
- Will it distract from, rather than enhance, my argument?
- What sort of text will I need to write to place the video in context?
- Have I given full and proper credit for the video if someone else created it?

Sound

In the early days of the Internet, web pages were sometimes accompanied by a cheesy MIDI soundtrack, which was so annoying that the average user fled the page immediately. Even if Musical Instrument Digital Interface is long before your time, remember that a little sound goes a long way.

If you've recorded an interview, you might use snippets in a digital essay, similar to the way you'd present a video interview. You might use music, but again, do so briefly and subtly. A podcast, too, can serve as compelling evidence for your argument, but don't link to a one-hour file and expect your instructor to listen to the entire program.

In general, you should allow a sentence spoken aloud about the same amount of space and time you would allot to a written sentence. Think how long your own patience lasts when you're surfing the web: if something isn't immediately compelling, you'll probably skip over it. As with video, your instructor will have limited patience for any use of sound that does not directly and meaningfully move your argument forward.

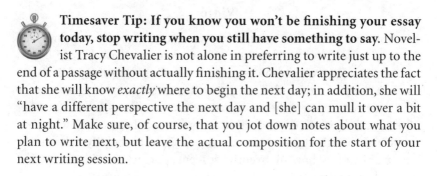 **Timesaver Tip: If you know you won't be finishing your essay today, stop writing when you still have something to say.** Novelist Tracy Chevalier is not alone in preferring to write just up to the end of a passage without actually finishing it. Chevalier appreciates the fact that she will know *exactly* where to begin the next day; in addition, she will "have a different perspective the next day and [she] can mull it over a bit at night." Make sure, of course, that you jot down notes about what you plan to write next, but leave the actual composition for the start of your next writing session.

Questions and Suggestions FOR You

1. Search your library's database for an expert's strongly worded *opinion* on your topic. Then search the database again, this time for concrete and persuasive *evidence* to support your topic. Write a passage that uses the evidence to support the expert's opinion.
2. Using the "quotation sandwich" format described above, quote from one of the articles you retrieved from your library's database.
3. Identify a local expert on your essay topic and request an interview. Prepare for the interview by learning more about the expert and writing a mixture of specific and general interview questions.
4. Write a short survey on your topic that can be answered by the members of your class. As with the interview, a combination of directed and open-ended questions will likely bring you the most satisfactory results.
5. Write a traditional academic paragraph on your topic. This will begin with 1) a topic sentence, and will be followed by 2) supporting evidence, 3) your analysis of that evidence, and 4) a concluding sentence.
6. Write a passage that contains narrative (storytelling) and uses description to bring to life an important element of your essay.
7. Choose a photograph or drawing to support your essay's central argument. Write a caption for the image, then write a paragraph, analyzing the the image.
8. Use a pie chart or bar graph to help readers visualize a significant numerical measure relevant to your essay. Be sure to include written text that explains and analyzes your visual.
9. In a short paragraph, describe the ideal short video for your essay and explain why such a video would help you persuade readers of the validity of your argument. If you are writing in a digital environment and your instructor thinks a video would help your essay, either find or create a video that matches the description in your paragraph.
10. Choose or create a sound file that you think will help strengthen one of your essay's main arguments. Then write a paragraph, analyzing the file.

Questions and Suggestions FROM You

List three questions you still have after reading this section. Start by reviewing the chapter. If that method doesn't inspire three questions, think about the overall topic of writing body paragraphs. What don't you know about the subject that you would still like to know?

1. _____

_____

_____

_____

_____

2. _____

_____

_____

_____

_____

3. _____

_____

_____

_____

_____

Describe one activity related to writing body paragraphs *not mentioned in this chapter* that you think would be helpful to do in class. Any successful activity in any course you've ever taken might serve as a model.

_____

_____

_____

_____

_____

CHAPTER EIGHT

Conclusion: Wait ... Don't Stop

CONCLUSION DOS AND DON'TS

If a strong introduction buys you goodwill with a reader, a strong conclusion may be even more important. Other than the Works Cited page documenting your sources, the conclusion is the last thing your instructor will read before awarding you a grade. Finishing on a positive note can mean the difference between a good and a *really* good grade.

Unfortunately, when you reach your conclusion, you're probably getting pretty tired of your essay. This short chapter urges you to resist the impulse to hurry through your conclusion as quickly as possible, and instead to give your closing sentences as much thought as you gave your opening hook. Whether you are envisioning your primary reader as a specific imaginary audience—the readers of a newspaper's opinion column, for instance, or the CEO of a corporation—or simply the instructor of your class, you will want to do everything possible to positively distinguish your essay from others like it.

It helps to take an extended break after writing the body of your essay and then come back to the conclusion with fresh eyes. However, if you're on a deadline, even a walk around the block can help reboot your imagination and energy.

A good way to tell whether your conclusion has any punch is to cut and paste it into a separate document and evaluate it without reference to the rest of the essay. When you are looking at your conclusion as a separate entity, ask yourself these questions:

- Does it stand on its own as a good piece of writing?
- Does it contain concrete and specific details, which readers normally find engaging, or is it composed mostly of abstractions and vague generalizations?

- Does it make you want to read the essay that preceded it?
- Did you *enjoy* writing it? (If not, readers probably won't enjoy reading it.)

Whatever approach you take to crafting your conclusion, you will want to remind your reader of the overall relevance of your topic. Imagine a reader who doesn't have much interest in what you are saying. This person is always asking *Who cares?* and *So what?* Give your reader reason to care about what you've just written.

As we consider some strategies for ending on a high note, let's imagine we are concluding an essay that was driven by the following thesis statement:

> While it may be too late to avoid climate change, it's not too late to diminish its effects. In order to do so, we must, as soon as possible, take the following steps: transition from gasoline-powered to electric cars; reduce our water consumption by 50% or more; and recycle *all the time*, not just when it's convenient.

What follows are lists of conclusion *Dos* and *Don'ts*, along with examples relevant to a hypothetical essay on climate change. If your conclusion feels thin, consider incorporating several of the *Dos*. If it feels flat, stale, and false, be sure you haven't fallen into the trap of the *Don'ts*.

CONCLUSION DOS AND DON'TS

Dos

Do Include a Persuasive Quotation from an Expert

As you research your topic, you will be collecting quotations from experts that you plan to use in the body paragraphs of your essay. As you compile these persuasive quotations, consider reserving one of the strongest for your concluding paragraph. Doing so helps keep your conclusion from feeling like an unimportant afterthought.

> As former vice-president Al Gore writes in his book, *The Future: Six Drivers of Global Change*, the evidence for climate change is "data-driven and is based on deep research and reporting—not speculation, alarmism, naïve optimism, or blue-sky conjecture." Gore concludes ominously, "There is no prior period of change that remotely resembles what humanity is about to experience."

Do Incorporate a Dramatic Statistic

The more striking the numbers, the more likely you will grab your reader's attention. Make sure, of course, that your statistic is from a credible source.

> According to the National Aeronautics and Space Administration (NASA), "Ninety-seven percent of climate scientists agree that climate-warming trends over the past century are very likely due to human activities, and most of the leading scientific organizations worldwide have issued public statements endorsing this position." There's no longer any doubt that climate change is occurring: the only question is how best to face it.

Do Issue a Modest and Reasonable Call to Action

If you have convincingly made the case for your thesis, your reader may well want to know what, specifically, she or he can do next. The more specific and practical you are in your recommendations, the more likely your readers will actually follow them.

> If you must own a car, the next time you buy one, purchase an electric vehicle. If you own a home in an area that receives little rainfall, replace your lawn with native, drought-resistant plants. Finally, keep recycling containers in every room in your home where trash is generated. These are small steps, but they *are* doable. And they can make a difference.

Do Use Narrative and Description

The previous chapter suggests ways to use "creative nonfiction" in the body of your essay. Review that section and consider telling a detailed and descriptive story in your conclusion. Immersing your readers in your topic one final time will make the topic feel vivid and real. If you decide to take this approach, be open to the possibility that your conclusion may be several paragraphs long.

> A six-year-old boy clings to a wooden pallet that floats through the city streets. The sewage smell would be overpowering if he weren't so used to it. He's hungry, thirsty, exhausted. His mother drowned in the most recent flood. He hasn't seen his father in years. The city is more water than land now, more the memory of a city than a place

where people actually live and work. Though it's noon, and very hot, the sky is dark. The first few drops of rain begin to fall. The boy considers letting go of the pallet and sliding into the dirty water. "Why bother?" he thinks. "Why bother at all?"

Science fiction? No. This is Bangladesh in the year 2050, if we don't begin to make the changes described in this essay.

Do Reconnect with Your Opening Hook

If you decide to reconnect with your opening hook, make sure that you extend, rather than simply repeat it. Imagine that the hook leading to the thesis statement above had focused on the dramatic increase in average annual temperatures around the globe. The return to your hook might reference escalating temperatures like this:

Every day that we do nothing, little by little, the mercury in our thermometers will continue to rise.

Don'ts

Reading uninspiring writing is, well ... *uninspiring.* It's crucial, therefore, that you make an effort not to finish your essay by simply typing the first thing that pops into your head. To give you a bit of insight into how instructors react to uninspiring writing, each example of a weak conclusion below is followed by the thought a professor might have in response.

Don't Simply Repeat What You've Already Said

Especially if your essay is just a few pages long, a highly repetitive conclusion makes it seem as though 1) your reader is incapable of remembering what she or he read just a few minutes ago, and 2) you have nothing else to add to your topic, so you are simply filling up space by restating old material.

The student writes:

In conclusion, I have made these three points: we must transition from gasoline-powered to electric cars, reduce our water consumption by 50% or more, and recycle *all the time,* not just when it's convenient.

The professor thinks:

How many times do I have to read to the phrase "In conclusion, I have made these three points . . ."? It's the last paragraph of the essay: *obviously* it's the conclusion. And by the way, isn't that sentence almost *identical* to the thesis?

Don't Be Boring

A boring conclusion often comes at the end of a boring essay, driving home the point that the writer has had nothing interesting to say about her or his topic. And even a good essay will be marred by a tedious ending. "Why," your instructor will want to know, "didn't you put as much effort into the conclusion as you did into the rest of the paper?"

The student writes:

Climate change is a problem that won't go away unless we do something about it. My essay has described some of the ways we can make changes. Therefore, these changes should be made as soon as possible. If we don't stop climate change, the world will become an unlivable place. We must do something about it today.

The professor thinks:

Coffee, anyone?

Don't Use a Random Quotation

While a relevant quotation from an expert on your topic is a compelling way to conclude an academic essay, using an arbitrary and barely applicable quotation that you found online at Brainyquotes or Bartelby.com suggests that you simply typed a keyword into a quotation-generator: in other words, you didn't put much time into locating the most appropriate concluding statement.

The student writes:

It is time to make a change when it comes to climate change. In the words of Plutarch, "I don't need a friend who changes when I change and who nods when I nod; my shadow does that much better."

The professor thinks:

Sigh.

Don't Claim to Have Done More in Your Essay than You Actually Did

You know the feeling: you've finished a draft of your essay and you realize you didn't accomplish what you set out to do. Rather than revising the essay so that the evidence in the body paragraphs support your thesis statement, you make a sweeping and unsubstantiated claim that your essay has done far more work than it really has.

The student writes:

> As I have conclusively proven, climate change is for real and the only way to avoid it is to follow the plan I have outlined in my essay.

The professor thinks:

> Wow, who needs scientific research now that we have your essay?

Don't Ask for the Impossible

If it's realistic to issue a reasonable and modest call for action, asking the impossible of your readers is likely to make them do nothing at all. Sure, it would be great if reading your essay would make your professor swear never again to ride in any vehicle powered by an internal combustion engine, but is that really going to happen? You're even less likely to move your reader if the call to action is phrased in extremely vague and general terms.

The student writes:

> Stop the use of all fossil fuels right now! Your life depends on it!

The professor thinks:

> And how am I supposed to do that again?

Don't Delay Your Thesis until the End...

... unless your professor specifically advises you to do so, of course. Otherwise, assume that your reader wants to know your topic up front so that she or he can accurately assess the strength of your arguments and evidence.

 Timesaver Tip: Give yourself extra time to complete your essay. Every once in a while, we "burn with a hard, gem-like flame," to quote the Victorian writer Walter Pater, and are able to do excellent work in a short amount of time. More often, though, our writing is like a fountain with an iffy water supply. Sometimes it's working. Other times it's not. Adding a few extra days into your writing schedule will reduce your stress levels and result in a stronger essay.

Questions and Suggestions FOR You

1. Print out a draft of your essay, *without* the conclusion. Then open a new document and write the conclusion as though it were a separate assignment. Revert to the list of *Dos* to strengthen your final paragraph. Try writing something that you would enjoy reading yourself.
2. If you have already written your conclusion, make sure it doesn't commit any of the "sins" in the *Don'ts* list. Excise problem areas and substitute them with appropriate suggestions from the *Dos* section.

Questions and Suggestions FROM You

List three questions you still have after reading this section. Start by reviewing the chapter. If that method doesn't inspire three questions, think about the overall topic of writing conclusions. What don't you know about the subject that you would still like to know?

1. _____

_____

_____

_____

_____

2. _____

_____

_____

_____

3. _____

_____

_____

_____

_____

Describe one activity related to writing conclusions *not mentioned in this chapter* that you think would be helpful to do in class. Any successful activity in any course you've ever taken might serve as a model.

_____

_____

_____

_____

_____

PART THREE: GO AGAIN

CHAPTER NINE

Taking Another Look

REVISION
EDITING

REVISION

"Shitty first drafts," Anne Lamott calls our early writing efforts, and most of us know exactly what she means. In her book *Bird by Bird* she claims, "All good writers write them. This is how they end up with good second drafts and terrific third drafts."

Therefore, while you may think, after writing your concluding paragraph, "I'm done!" don't be so sure. If unrevised first drafts represented the average student's best work even *some* of the time, many instructors would be willing to back down on the need for revision. However, that's just not true. In their venerable textbook *The Elements of Style*, William Strunk and E.B. White caution that "Few writers are so expert they can produce what they are after on the first try." Most professional writers are avid revisers of their own work, and if someone who has been getting paid for her or his writing for decades still feels the need to go over it numerous times, don't you, as a novice academic writer, have the same responsibility?

Revision literally means "re-seeing," and that's what taking another look is all about. This chapter was initially titled "Revision: The Fun Stuff." I changed it because I thought students would think I was being ironic, but I wasn't. For me, at least, writing the first draft is always the most difficult step. Filling the blank page with words is daunting. However, once those words are on the page, the task of rearranging them and replacing them with others is not unlike putting a puzzle together. Revision is essentially problem-solving, and while you may be better at solving problems in math than in English, you can still apply some of the same evaluative and analytic skills to make your writing stronger.

Even an author like Lisa Schroeder, who doesn't necessarily relish the revision process, finds some satisfaction in it. She compares revision to cleaning your room, "because it may not be fun while you're doing it, but when you're finished, you can stand back and see what you've done, and think, 'Wow! That looks great!'"

Normally, you want to give yourself some time between your completed first draft and your first revision. Ideally, you would have a day or more of allowing your thoughts to settle and for you to become less devoted to your first draft. However, even an hour of exercise, music, or doing nothing at all can help you see your essay in a new light.

Donald Murray argues in his book *A Writer Teaches Writing* that professional writers scrutinize their own work by returning to it over and over: "The writer reads and rereads and rereads, standing far back and reading quickly from a distance, moving in close and reading slowly line by line, reading again and again, knowing that the answers to all writing problems lie within the evolving text."

Academic Writing Now is here to give you suggestions for how to approach the revision of your essay, but the more accustomed you become to the process, the more you will be like the writers Murray describes, turning to your own work again and again to see what works and what doesn't, what is missing and what needs to go.

Global vs. Local Issues

Revision involves looking at the big picture, at "global issues" like the overall argument and structure of the essay. Editing, on the other hand, tends to take place on the sentence level: while you're fairly confident the essay is sound, you know it's not yet ready for that final polishing. Proofreading, which we'll cover in the next chapter, is simply a matter of making sure that what you thought you'd written is actually on the page. It's important to proofread, but if you do so before or without addressing revision and editing concerns, you are basically wasting your precious time on an activity that will not result in a stronger essay or a better grade.

Writing professor Nancy Sommers believes that "at the heart of revision is the process by which writers recognize and resolve the dissonance they sense in their writing." Something doesn't sound right. An example you'd thought would support your thesis turns out to work against it. Material you thought was crucial when you began is, in fact, just clogging things up and needs to go.

When talking about the difference between drafting and revising, composition textbooks often refer to writing theorist Peter Elbow's believing and doubting games. According to Elbow, when you begin writing, you want to play the believing game. That is, you try and suspend your judgment of yourself, and instead get creative. You explore, play, generate. You don't stop writing just because something isn't perfect.

However, once you have reached a point where you're considering letting an audience read your work, you need to play the doubting game. You become the skeptic, disinclined to believe anything unless it is supported by persuasive evidence. You try and read your work as though it were written by someone else.

Of course, it's impossible to entirely shut out this back and forth between believing and doubting during either drafting or revision. Nevertheless, having completed a first draft, you will want to begin moving from coach to critic, from defense lawyer to judge.

Revising a Sample Draft

Once again, let's focus our discussion by envisioning a sample assignment, this time one with a full first draft attached. Here's an essay prompt for one of my assignments:

> *Assignment Prompt*: Write an essay that critiques a specific form of social media—Facebook, Twitter, Reddit, Snapchat, etc. Even if you find certain aspects of your particular social media beneficial, the essay's focus should be on those areas you find most troubling, especially for college-aged students. While you may use some personal experience to support your thesis, the majority of your evidence should come from experts in the field. (Cite at least five secondary sources using MLA-style documentation.) As you know, social media changes all the time, so be sure your research is as current as possible. Your essay should be between 1000 and 1500 words, not including your Works Cited page.

And here's a response by one of my students:

Problems with Facebook
by
Caroline Stubbs

Should we be concerned about some of the problems associated with Facebook? As a parent, Michael Duffy thinks so. He worries about the way many teens seem to have an illusion of privacy on the site.

He also has concerns about Facebook's "darker passages," such as "defamatory speech," cyber-bullying and stalking. However, he says what troubles him most is the fact that kids waste so much time on this network. Though I agree with Duffy that we should be concerned about Facebook, I worry more about the lack of privacy and the "dark sides" than about wasting time.

Duffy points out that teens seem to "think their lives are private" on the site, "as long as their parents aren't tuning in." This is a real problem. In high school, I had friends who posted pictures of themselves at parties drunk all the time. It created so many problems. For example, our soccer coach heard rumors that we were drinking and there is a zero tolerance policy for drinking on the team. If a player is caught with alcohol, she is automatically off the team. My senior year, one player, who didn't get much field time, showed the coach a Facebook picture of other players partying. At that point, our coach had to follow through, even if he didn't want to. Three of our best players got kicked off the team, which meant we lost in the first round of CIF. When I asked my friends what they were thinking when they posted those pictures, they just said, "We never thought an adult would see them!" They just saw Facebook as a "teens only environment," which is how Facebook presents itself.

Duffy also comments briefly on the "dark side" of Facebook. This is the part of Facebook that concerns me most. Facebook presents an ideal environment for bullies and stalkers. Teens with no impulse control can write things that are cruel and hurtful on Facebook and then somehow feel more anonymous when they do it. They can spread hateful rumors that are so difficult to overcome, especially when they are in print. Duffy wrote his article in 2006, but I think cyber-bullying is even more of a problem now. We hear about a case on the news almost daily. Facebook is also an ideal place for stalkers to operate. Though we have laws against someone physically stalking you, it's hard to monitor what another person does online. After I broke up with my high school boyfriend, he sent endless messages to my Facebook account. When I blocked him, he started doing the same to my friends. He would even create "fake" accounts and try to friend request me. It was never ending! I started using Facebook less and Snapchat more, which is a pretty common decision for people these days. Facebook needs to take some responsibility for this problem, because it is providing a forum for individuals who are mentally unstable with a bad (sometimes violent) intent toward someone else.

Finally, Duffy says he's most upset about time wasting on Facebook. He even calls Facebook a "time vortex." To me, it depends on how the user is spending the time on Facebook that matters most. I might spend an hour writing a long message to my father who lives across the country, and that is time well spent. Keeping up with friends I don't see is also, in my view, time well spent. However, if I am stalking another person, putting up cruel messages or posting photos of myself drunk, then that is another matter. I don't think Duffy can say the time is wasted until he makes it clear exactly what is being done during that time.

Duffy raises some important concerns about Facebook. I share his concerns, though my priorities are different from his. I see some positive aspects of Facebook, but I also think the company needs to step up and protect users from bullies and stalkers. Facebook also needs to educate its young users about privacy, because those "fun" photos might just come back to haunt you some day.

Rereading the Prompt

Professors grade essays based on the assignments they have given their students. You may not like the assignment, but you must follow it if you hope to earn a good grade. Therefore, the first thing to do when you are ready to sit down and revise your essay is to reread the essay prompt.

Many professors include a grading rubric showing how each part of the prompt will be graded and how much weight it will be given. This assignment has no rubric, but the prompt is extremely specific. Caroline does focus on the prompt to an extent: she critiques a specific form of social media and provides concrete and detailed examples to support each of her main points. So far, so good.

However, the prompt also states, "While you may use some personal experience to support your thesis, the majority of your evidence should come from experts in the field." The prompt goes on to say that students must "Cite at least five secondary sources using MLA-style documentation" and recommends that the "research is as current as possible." There's a problem here: almost all of Caroline's supporting examples are drawn from personal experience. Moreover, her research consists of a single article, "Gen-M: A Dad's Encounter with the Vortex of Facebook," published in the March 19, 2006, edition of *Time* magazine. And while she mentions Duffy's name and the subject of his essay, we never hear the exact title or the essay's source.

Based on Caroline's essay, Duffy's article sounds as though it is mostly an opinion piece (and that turns out to be true). If Duffy includes solid evidence to support his opinions, we can't tell that from the quotations Caroline provides.

Because *no* aspect of a writing prompt is irrelevant, a revision of "Problems with Facebook" will require Caroline to make significant changes to her first draft. In order to make sure she covers everything, I suggested that she look at each requirement as a separate sentence, reformatting the prompt in bullet form with important points in bold, like this:

- **Write an essay that critiques a specific form of social media**—Facebook, Twitter, Reddit, Snapchat, etc.
- Even if you find certain aspects of your particular social media beneficial, **the essay's focus should be on those areas you find most troubling, especially for college-aged students.**
- While you may use some personal experience to support your thesis, **the majority of your evidence should come from experts in the field.**
- **Cite at least five secondary sources** using **MLA-style documentation.**
- As you know, social media changes all the time, so **be sure your research is as current as possible.**
- Your essay should be **between 1000 and 1500 words**, not including your Works Cited page.

Simply taking the prompt apart like this can make it easier to understand, analyze, and respond to.

Avoid This Common Error: Wishful thinking. Often when we've forgotten to do something others expected of us, we simply cross our fingers that they will forget. Don't make that mistake when responding to your essay prompt. Ignoring crucial directions in an assignment will result in a significantly lower grade for your essay.

Follow-Up Research

The good thing about a first draft, of course, is that it doesn't receive a grade. In her revision, Caroline will need to focus, first, on research. If she is to follow the prompt, she will need some current and reliable secondary sources to bolster her personal claims. Finding relevant research and citing authoritative sources will also help her reach the minimum word count without padding her essay.

Based on the content of her second and third paragraphs, Caroline's focus should probably be on researching the negative consequences of posting inappropriate pictures on Facebook and the sometimes devastating results of cyberbullying.

What's important to remember here is how often you are likely to return to the research process. If you follow the model outlined in this book, you will do "lightning research" when you first know your assignment, then much more thorough research after you have crafted a working thesis statement and an outline. But research doesn't end there. You come back to it in the revision process, and you may continue to search for and confirm credible sources as you move into the editing and even proofreading stages.

New research is very likely to shift the focus of your thesis and essay, either slightly or significantly, so you need to be open to that possibility. As researchers Linda Flower and John Hayes eloquently put it, by setting new goals during the revising process, "the fruits of discovery come back to inform the continuing process of writing."

Organization

Lisa Schroeder's comparison of revision to reorganizing a messy room won't work for everyone, but it does point out the necessity of moving things around, of throwing out junk and possibly bringing in new items to suit the overall *feng shui* of the freshly created space.

One time-tested way of seeing just how much reorganization will be required is to print out your draft and mark it with a pen or a pencil. While you might worry that this is a waste of paper and printer ink, a hard copy nearly always allows you to see things you missed when the essay was only on your computer screen. As you read, ask yourself: "Have I accomplished what I set out to do in this essay? If not, what work still needs to be done?"

A **reverse outline**, the same tool that helped you analyze readings, can also work to tighten your organization. Remember that in a reverse outline (described in Chapter 2) you look at *what is actually on the page*, and write an outline that identifies the thesis, topic sentences, and main pieces of supporting evidence. Reverse outlining your own essay forces you to see what you've actually written, rather than what you'd thought was there or what you'd hoped to write.

Sometimes the order of the body paragraphs seems obvious. Maybe, for instance, you are discussing your topic in chronological fashion, so it makes sense to start with the earliest material and end with the most recent.

However, if you have three equally relevant, but basically separate, paragraphs, and you're not sure how to organize them, consider this formula: 2, 3, 1, where 1 is the strongest paragraph and 3 is the weakest. Ideally, of course, all your paragraphs are equally wonderful, but if that's not the case, it's best to start fairly strong, sandwich your least convincing argument in the middle, and then finish with your strongest paragraph, near the point when your reader (and grader) is making a final assessment of your work.

As in the initial stages of the drafting process, your essay's organization should be shaped by your thesis statement. Reread your thesis and ask yourself:

- Does my thesis still work for the essay?
- Does it need to be revised? If so, how much?
- If the thesis still seems persuasive and arguable, do I need to revise my body paragraphs instead?

Caroline's essay is organized around the easy-to-follow traditional five-paragraph structure. Her thesis is serviceable, if unspectacular. A complete revision of the essay's organization is probably not necessary, although considerable work remains to be done within the paragraphs themselves.

Overwriting and Underwriting

Author Stephen King has a formula: "2nd Draft = 1st Draft – 10%." If you tend to overwrite, you will want to do what King does: take out unnecessary words and phrases. Early drafts often contain a good deal of redundancy. You have an idea. You state it one way. Then you state the same idea slightly differently. And, just to make sure your reader gets the picture, you make a few adjustments and write the same idea yet again. Obviously, you only need one version of that idea—the clearest, most succinct expression of it.

Redundancies aside, if, while rereading your draft, you are seized by the desire to delete something, you should probably save it elsewhere—in another file, or on a separate page at the bottom of your document. Frequently, an idea or sentence that seems unnecessary in one draft turns out to be quite useful later on. Nevertheless, don't hesitate to move text around or to get rid of it altogether. Remember the words of Pablo Picasso: "The urge to destroy is also a creative urge."

If you don't feel that you're being wordy, but your draft is still too long for your assignment, make sure all of your paragraphs are necessary. Sometimes an idea that you initially thought was valuable doesn't really fit into the finished version of your draft. Other times, you may be able to combine and condense two related paragraphs.

For many writers, though, the second draft is a time to add at least as much material as they subtract. Because your essay's overall organization should support the main points in your thesis statement, it's worth looking back at the topic sentences in your outline. Does your essay provide sufficient and convincing evidence for each one?

If your draft is *under*developed, remember some of the ideas described in Chapter 7 for creating fully realized internal paragraphs:

- Include direct quotations from experts that are preceded by signal phrases and followed by your commentary.
- Conduct an interview or a survey, then show and discuss the results.
- Tell a relevant story using appeals to all five senses (sight, sound, smell, touch, and taste).
- Employ—and explain—charts, tables, images, video, and sound.

Caroline Stubbs's "Problems with Facebook" already includes a good deal of storytelling. Instead, her revised body paragraphs will need to focus more on factual material.

 Timesaver Tip: Go to the Writing Center. Again. Any time during the writing process is a good time to discuss what you've done and what you still need to do to make your essay as strong as possible. However, you're likely to get the most valuable feedback when you've completed a full first draft.

Peer Review

Bringing in a draft for peer review can be daunting. What if the other students don't like your essay? What if they make fun of it? What if everyone else seems smarter than you? If it's any comfort, millions of students before you have had precisely the same fears. Fortunately, there are ways to avoid a counterproductive session.

Before you bring your essay in for peer review:

- Read it out loud.
- Let someone else read it.
- Describe it to someone else, paragraph by paragraph.
- If you have time, consider writing another draft: peer response tends to be more useful the closer a draft is to completion.

Creating a positive environment in your peer writing group is essential. Try to follow these basic guidelines:

- Be polite. Treat others the way you would like to be treated.
- Be prepared. The person who hasn't read the work or doesn't understand the assignment is a drain on the group. If you are that person, you can obviously benefit a great deal from a small-group discussion, but it's not the responsibility of your fellow group members to bring you up to speed.
- Be specific in your comments. Rather than saying, "I thought your essay was kind of vague," point to particular paragraphs and sentences that could be strengthened through the use of concrete supporting examples.
- If you are a more accomplished writer than the student whose work is being discussed, be a generous mentor.
- If you are a less accomplished writer than the student whose work is being discussed, be a listener and a learner, but do comment on issues you feel need the student's attention.
- When your essay is under discussion, listen to everyone. Be open to receiving useful feedback from classmates you may not personally like, but who have good ideas. Likewise, don't always listen to your friends' advice: it may not be as astute as that of someone who doesn't know you.

Of course, when the writer is sitting right there among you, you may be hesitant to offer a critique that could hurt his or her feelings. However, in order to truly help that person craft a better piece of writing, you must be willing to make polite, constructive suggestions.

Peer Review Questions

The following questions will usually result in a productive peer review session. Be sure your group illustrates its discussion with specific examples from the student's essay.

- What is the essay's thesis? Is it specific and arguable?
- What are the main points of the essay? Is each one worth arguing?
- Are the body paragraphs supported by concrete, specific, and convincing evidence? If not, what evidence is needed and where?
- Are the introduction and conclusion interesting and thoughtful? If not, what can the writer do to make them more compelling?
- If the prompt indicates the essay should be directed at a specific audience, how well has the writer addressed that audience?
- Where do you find yourself most interested?
- Where do you find yourself most bored?
- Where do you find yourself most confused?
- What *one* question about the topic would you still like the writer to answer?

Though questions like these are helpful, a peer review session should always be open to change. If an essay has one *huge* problem—a missing thesis statement, for example, or a paragraph that undercuts the entire argument—it's a waste of time to focus on re-crafting the opening hook until the group addresses those larger issues. Think of yourself as a paramedic arriving at the scene of an accident: as quickly as possible, identify the most urgent issues and address them first.

In the case of Caroline's draft, her peer review group spent most of its time helping her identify and locate the expert sources she needed to support her argument. Group members were on their phones and laptops, chatting amiably as they batted around research ideas.

Avoid This Common Error: Wasting time in a peer review group. Everyone who's ever participated in a peer writing group has probably had at least one unproductive experience, with the students rushing through the draft as quickly as possible. If your group is floundering, take charge. You may think you'll have plenty of other opportunities for people to look at your work, so why not goof off a bit? However, there are always fewer opportunities and less time for revision than you think there will be. Successful students take advantage of any opportunity to make their time count.

Revision Checklist

Revision is an ongoing and complex process, so no single checklist can ask you *every* question about your essay that you might need to answer. However, if you can reply in the affirmative to the following questions, and you have the material in your essay to back it up, you are probably well on your way toward completing your revision:

- Does your essay meet *all* the requirements of the prompt? In particular, are you writing to the audience designated by the assignment?
- Is the opening paragraph engaging and does it provide a clear sense of the overall scope of the essay?
- Is the thesis clear, arguable, and capable of sustaining a full-length essay?
- Does your thesis accurately reflect what is actually in the essay?
- Have you avoided stating the obvious?
- Does each body paragraph have a clear topic sentence?
- Does each body paragraph support its topic sentence with concrete, detailed, appropriate, and persuasive specific examples?

- Do you intelligently analyze and comment on the evidence in each body paragraph?
- Have you considered including multimodal examples (visuals, sound, video) that will further persuade your reader of the validity of your argument? If you have made multimodal moves, are they well integrated into the rest of your essay?
- Is your conclusion compelling?
- Are you proud enough of your essay to ask a friend or relative to read it?

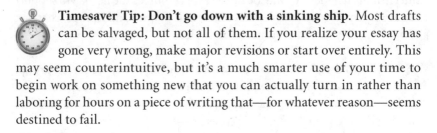 **Timesaver Tip: Don't go down with a sinking ship**. Most drafts can be salvaged, but not all of them. If you realize your essay has gone very wrong, make major revisions or start over entirely. This may seem counterintuitive, but it's a much smarter use of your time to begin work on something new that you can actually turn in rather than laboring for hours on a piece of writing that—for whatever reason—seems destined to fail.

EDITING

Cultural critic Clive James admits, "I work on the assumption, or let it be fear, that the reader will stop reading if I stop being interesting." Students don't normally worry about being dull in an academic essay—but maybe they should. Granted, professors can't really stop reading just because something is boring; after all, grading essays is part of an instructor's job. However, a poorly written essay will make a reader who wishes he or she had stopped reading feel very cranky just before awarding the essay a grade. Better by far to try and emulate James, who attempts "to make every sentence as attractive as the first."

As you turn from revising to editing, and attempt to make your sentences as "attractive" as possible, you'll begin tackling issues of grammar and style: two of the most challenging facets of writing. Indeed, many very long books have been written on these two aspects of academic writing. If you find yourself confounded by a particular issue, you may want to consult a grammar and style handbook (currently, both the University of Minnesota and the University of Illinois offer excellent—and free—online versions), but you will almost certainly want to talk about the problem with your instructor or a tutor. Often, an experienced writer can explain a concept in a few minutes that you may puzzle over for hours on your own.

Still, though it's impossible to cover all aspects of grammar and style in a book as short as this one, it's nevertheless worth looking at a few of the most common problems student writers encounter as they edit their essays.

Grammar

We'll look first at grammar, a word that is applied to everything from the study of an entire system of language to the use of the proper verb with the correct noun to the proper placement of a comma. To help you negotiate the complex rules of writing, your instructor may well have assigned a grammar and style handbook along with *Academic Writing Now*. If not, turn to one of the sites listed above, or to Purdue's Online Writing Lab, or to one of the publisher sites you'll find when searching for "online grammar handbook."

With each updated version, word-processing programs feature more and more sophisticated grammar checks, and running a grammar check on your essay is never a bad idea. That said, don't blindly make a change just because your computer draws a green line under a word or sentence. Consider *why* the program is making the suggestion and whether you have a better understanding of your sentence than your software's algorithm.

Frequent Errors

You can get a head start on eliminating errors by being especially aware of the following mistakes frequently made by first-year writing students.

Commas

If you've been told you are prone to making comma errors, it's worth having a sit-down with your professor or a tutor: the number of ways in which a comma can be misused is astounding. However, the most frequent errors are forgetting to put a comma where one was needed (for instance, before a conjunction like "but" or "and"), or inserting a comma where it was not necessary.

Comma Splice

In this common error, the writer uses a comma to join two independent clauses (i.e., two complete sentences). Good grammar, however, requires a coordinating conjunction ("and," "but," "or," etc.) after the comma. You may also substitute the comma with a period, semicolon, colon, or dash.

> *Not this*: My life has had many twists and turns, I always come out on top.
> *But this*: My life has had many twists and turns, but I always come out on top.
> *Or this*: My life has had many twists and turns. I always come out on top.

Run-on or Fused Sentence

This is another punctuation error involving independent clauses, and a close cousin of the comma splice. This time, however, the writer has left punctuation out altogether between the two complete sentences. Once again, the writer needs a coordinating conjunction, or a period, semicolon, colon, or dash. Note: Students often use "run-on" to mean an overly long sentence, but grammatically that's inaccurate. A sentence can be pages long and still, grammatically speaking, *not* be a run-on.

> *Not this*: The last thing we do is often the best the first thing is the hardest.
> *But this*: The last thing we do is often the best; the first thing is the hardest.
> *Or this*: The last thing we do is often the best, yet the first thing is the hardest.

Fragment

Another punctuation error. (The previous sentence is a fragment by the way: it has no subject or verb.) In the case of a fragment, what the writer thinks can stand alone as a sentence actually can't, from a grammatical standpoint. Technically, a fragment is a dependent clause separated from its independent clause. Typically, a fragment should be connected by a comma to the preceding sentence, although that's not always the case.

> *Not this*: The greatest guitar player ever. Jimi Hendrix shredded his way through "Voodoo Chile."
> *But this*: The greatest guitar player ever, Jimi Hendrix shredded his way through "Voodoo Chile."

Apostrophe

If your instructor has marked an apostrophe error on your rough draft, you most likely 1) have an apostrophe in the wrong place, 2) don't have an apostrophe when you should have one, or 3) have an apostrophe when it's not necessary. Often, this is an error that you will immediately know how to correct once someone points it out. You will recall that apostrophes are typically used for possession, not plurals, and that you should avoid the common mix-up of "it's" and "its."

Not this: Tomorrow is it's final day.
But this: Tomorrow is its final day.

Dash vs. Hyphen

A dash (—) is different from a hyphen (-). A dash is a punctuation mark, similar to a colon or a comma. A hyphen is used to divide or combine individual words.

Dash: I can't stand this heat—not anymore.
Hyphen: Even though that model is accident-prone, she's still camera-ready.

Wrong Word

If your instructor marks "wrong word" on your draft, the word you have chosen is inaccurate; it does not function in the way the sentence requires.

Not this: I past the store yesterday.
But this: I passed the store yesterday.

Spelling

A spelling error usually occurs in a word-processing document for two reasons: 1) you forgot to run a spellcheck, or 2) you ran spellcheck and changed a wrong word into a correctly spelled word that was, however, not the one you intended to use.

Redundancy

Instructors use the word "redundant" to indicate when students are needlessly repeating material. Basically, the message is this: "You've already said this, so you don't need to say it again."

Tense Shift

Like apostrophe errors, tense shifts are often the result of quick and careless writing. Somewhere in the middle of a paragraph or sentence you have changed the tense from the one you were using initially—from past to present, or vice versa. Once you choose a tense in your essay, be consistent throughout, unless of course a tense shift makes logical sense.

Titles

As we saw in Chapter 7, the titles of longer works, like books and films, should be *italicized*. The titles of shorter works—such as short stories, poems, and songs—go inside quotation marks. The first, last, and all "major" words in a title are capitalized. Unless they are the first or last words, articles and conjunctions are usually in lower case.

Then/Than, Lose/Loose, Anyway/Anyways

"Then" shows cause and effect or the passage of time: "He left, and *then* she left." "Than" indicates comparison and difference: "He's bigger *than* she is."

"Lose" is a verb: "Don't *lose* your shirt." "Loose" is an adjective: "That shirt looks *loose* on you."

In Standard Written English you should use "anyway," not the colloquial "anyways."

Grammar Log

Of course, the errors listed above are just a sampling of where a sentence can go wrong. Indeed, one of the challenges of teaching and learning grammar is that different people are prone to making different errors.

A time-efficient way of tracking and eliminating your own errors is to keep a grammar log. Early in the semester, before you've received your first graded paper, you may have to rely on your own memories of the types of errors you've made in the past. However, once you begin receiving graded essays, you can keep a careful record of your mistakes and put an end to them as quickly as possible.

Tutors can also help you identify and understand mistakes, and if you visit your instructor during office hours, she or he may point out frequently occurring problems. While it can take any form you wish, a Grammar Log often looks something like this:

Incorrect Sentence	Name of Grammar Error	Corrected Sentence
They is cold.	Subject-Verb Agreement	They are cold.
Its my house.	Missing Apostrophe	It's my house.
Where, will I be tomorrow?	Unnecessary Comma	Where will I be tomorrow?

The simple act of writing or typing out an error, naming it, and then correcting it can be surprisingly effective in helping you recognize a similar error in your next essay. It's also quite satisfying to realize that an error you once made almost without thinking has now been eradicated from your writing.

Style

Style, which essentially means "a way of doing something," is a more slippery concept than grammar. The famous trumpeter Louis Armstrong is supposed to have said, "If you have to ask what jazz is, you'll never know," and the same might be said for style.

Nevertheless, most of us recognize style, and in academic writing we can at least sketch some acceptable parameters. In college courses, you want to come across as intelligent without sounding pompous, and straightforward without sounding simplistic. "The way to speak and write what shall not go out of fashion is, to speak and write sincerely," Ralph Waldo Emerson wrote in his essay "Spiritual Laws." To sincerity, we might add the qualities of clarity and accuracy.

"Style," our old friend Aristotle said, "to be good must be clear.... Clearness is secured by using the words (nouns and verbs alike) that are current and ordinary." We hear a version of this emphasis on plain speech centuries later in book entitled *The King's English*, published in 1906:

- Prefer the familiar word to the far-fetched.
- Prefer the concrete word to the abstract.
- Prefer the simple word to the circumlocution.
- Prefer the short word to the long.

Of course, any set of rules is made to be broken. There *are* times when a long, abstract word may be preferable to a short, concrete one. Yet it's good to know that over a century ago, writing teachers were telling their students pretty much what writing teachers tell their students today: say what you have to say as precisely as possible.

Another element of style is what we might call the "music" of writing. Author Bebe Moore Campbell says she is "always looking for rhythm, looking for a click in my head. I listen to a lot of music. I am passionate about a lot of singers, and I try to infuse my books with the passion that the best singers had." Fiction writer Michael Chabon describes a similar experience: "When I'm writing, I'm also listening. I'll hear a rhythm; a pattern will beat in my mind that will encapsulate what I'm trying to say. Then the words will pop in."

As you revise for style, remember that while short simple sentences have impact, more than two or three in a row tend to make it appear as though you're incapable of writing something longer. Complex sentences, on the other hand, allow you to examine an idea in more depth and demonstrate your skill as a writer; yet these, too, can be overwhelming for a reader, and they are far more likely to result in grammatical errors.

Therefore, mix it up. When you need to make a clear point, go short and sharp. When you must step back and explain or provide context, longer sentences tend to work better.

We often value writers (and all creative people) as much for *how* they say something as for *what* they say. Yet in academic writing the *how* and the *what* are inextricably linked. In the words of author John Updike: "Style as I understand it is nothing less than the writer's habit of mind—it is not a kind of paint applied afterwards, but the very germ of the thing."

Slow Down

Academic Writing Now is subtitled *A Brief Guide for Busy Students*, but its ultimate aim is to get you to write efficiently, not carelessly. If you come to the point in the editing of your essay when you're seeing things you know are wrong but letting them go anyway, stop for a moment. Take a breath. Then return to your editing with a slower, more deliberate pace.

For nonfiction writer John McPhee, reading his work aloud is a crucial element in slowing things down so he will know when a piece is complete. "I can't stand a sentence until it sounds right," McPhee says, "and I'll go over it again and again." The next step for McPhee is to make sure that Sentence A and Sentence B work together as a unit: "One of the long-term things about knitting a piece of writing together is making all this stuff fit." If reading your essay aloud can help you *hear* where major revisions might be made, it is even more useful as a method for making sentence-level modifications. Try these tips for reading slowly as you turn to the editing of your essay:

- Physically point to each word as you read it.
- Put extra spaces between each of your sentences so that they stand alone physically, allowing you to focus more attention on each one.
- Read "backwards." Take a sheet of paper and cover up everything but the final sentence of your essay. Read that last sentence, focusing on grammar and style. Then read the next-to-last sentence, and so on, until you get to the first sentence.

Avoiding Biased Language

In general, today's students are far more culturally sensitive than their predecessors. Studies show that, while significant problems persist across North America, students are less racist, sexist, and homophobic than ever before.

Nevertheless, it's easy—especially if you are a heterosexual white male—to write as though everyone else in the world were exactly like you. Those who have traditionally held power have had a disproportionate influence on language, as on everything else. Therefore, as you go back and edit your essay, be sure you haven't inadvertently offended potential readers. Common sense works best, of course: put yourself in other people's shoes and imagine how they would react to your writing.

In addition to using your own good judgment, here are a few guidelines worth following:

- Never assume your reader is the same race or gender as you are, even if you know that the primary reader of your work is your instructor.
- Whenever possible, use the plural noun: "instructors" rather than "instructor."
- When you must use a singular pronoun, use "she or he" rather than "he."
- When appropriate, use the second-person pronoun: "You will write well" rather than "He will write well."
- Use "person" or "human" instead of "man": "humanity" rather than "mankind," "chairperson" rather than "chairman," and so on.

Editing Checklist

As with revision, no single editing checklist can cover every area of potential concern. This one is merely meant to get you started:

- Have you run a grammar check and spellcheck on the document (knowing, of course, that not every green or red underline will need to be corrected)?
- Have you checked for the types of errors first-year students frequently make (comma splices, fragments, wrong words, etc.)?
- If you are keeping a grammar log, have you searched for the errors you tended to make in the past?
- Do you have clear transitions between each of your paragraphs?
- Have you omitted needless words and sentences?

- Have you reread your essay slowly and carefully, pausing to consider possible solutions whenever you hear a potential problem?
- Are you using culturally sensitive language? That is, have you eliminated potentially offensive words and phrases?

Questions and Suggestions FOR You

1. Break your essay prompt into separate sentences or phrases, and then reread your essay to make sure you have covered the main points of your assignment.
2. It's the rare essay that can't be strengthened by more supporting evidence. Spend some time doing follow-up research on your topic.
3. Write a reverse outline of the current draft of your essay: reread what you have actually written, and write an outline that identifies the thesis, topic sentences, and main pieces of supporting evidence.
4. Print out a draft of your essay. Be sure you only have one paragraph per page (even if you have to momentarily change the spacing or the font). Then physically rearrange the paragraphs. Are you beginning with strong material and ending with your very best paragraph? If your original organization doesn't work, consider shuffling, adding, or deleting body paragraphs.
5. Print out three or four copies of your essay, then organize a small group of readers—whether it is your classmates, friends, or family—who are willing to give you written and oral feedback on your work.
6. Create a Grammar Log of your most frequent errors. If you haven't yet received any feedback from your instructor or a tutor, try to remember the types of errors you've commonly made in the past.
7. Print out a copy of your newly revised essay. Read the essay out loud, slowly, pointing to each word as you read. Mark the errors that you still need to address before you turn your essay in.

Questions and Suggestions FROM You

List three questions you still have after reading this section. Start by reviewing the chapter. If that method doesn't inspire three questions, think about the overall topic of revision and editing. What don't you know about the subject that you would still like to know?

1. _____

_____

_____

_____

_____

2. _____

_____

_____

_____

3. _____

_____

_____

_____

_____

Describe one activity related to revision and editing *not mentioned in this chapter* that you think would be helpful to do in class. Any successful activity in any course you've ever taken might serve as a model.

_____

_____

_____

_____

_____

CHAPTER TEN

Handing It Over

DESIGN AND PRESENTATION
PROOFREADING
TITLES
CAROLINE'S REVISION
KNOWING WHEN TO STOP

DESIGN AND PRESENTATION

As I suggested earlier, whatever your academic major, when you turn in an essay, you are essentially involved in a sales pitch. However, rather than landing a big contract, you are hoping to receive an "A" for your work.

Most of your grade will be awarded for the content of your essay: all the hard work we've covered in the previous chapters. However, you can enhance that effort by giving your essay a final polishing, just as you can lessen the essay's appeal by not attending to final details.

Designers use the word **layout**—the way in which the parts are arranged—to describe design and presentation. As you think about laying out your essay, it's helpful to remember that design and presentation are essentially methods of engaging your audience, of persuading them that the essay they are about to read, are reading, and have read, was carefully constructed—not only in terms of argument and organization, grammar and style—but also physically.

Audience really matters at this point. If your professor is Old School, with a distrust of fancy new bells and whistles, obviously you will want to be conservative in your use of unusual design elements. On the other hand, if your instructor has specifically talked about the importance of design elements—maybe even given you some tips on using images, video, or audio in a digital document—you'll probably want to apply these techniques in your own work.

Page 1

Unless your essay takes a radical digital format, it will necessarily begin with a first page. MLA style indicates that your first page should look like this:

Your Last Name 1

Your First and Last Name
Your Professor's Name
The Name of the Course
The Date You Are Submitting the Essay

The Essay's Title

The first line of the essay is indented and begins just one double-spaced lined below the title.

A few important design elements to register here:

- The entire document is double-spaced.
- The writer's last name appears in a header in the upper-right-hand corner of *every page*, with the appropriate page number one space after the last name.
- The writer's name, the professor's name, the name of the course, and the date the essay is being submitted are in the upper-left-hand corner just below the header, and are left-margin justified.
- The essay's title is centered and appears *two* double-spaced lines after the previous information.
- The first line of the essay is indented and begins just *one* double-spaced line after the title.
- The document should have margins of at least 1 inch or 2.5 centimeters.
- The right margin is "ragged" rather than right-margin justified.

Fonts

Times New Roman 12-point remains the default font for most academic essays. It's not flashy, but it's clear and easy to read. While it's fun to consider striking fonts like 𝓜𝓪𝓽𝓾𝓻𝓪 or **Braggadocio** or Noteworthy, in an academic essay it's easy to cross the line from attention-grabbing to silly—and no student about to receive a grade wants to be thought of as silly.

Headings

Throughout this book, I have used headings to make information easier to find and to break up the reading experience. Important headings are in red Small Caps. Secondary headings are in **bold**. Both of these headings are centered. The third-level heading is also in **bold**, but is left-margin justified. While a writer normally indents a new paragraph, I have followed the convention of keeping the first paragraph below a heading left-margin justified, with subsequent paragraphs indented as normal.

If you think headings will make your essay more readable, remember two simple rules:

Be consistent: However you use your headings, once you've decided on a pattern, you need to follow it all the way through your document. Any careless variation will disturb the sense of clarity and organization that headings help establish.

Be logical: The more important the section, the more attention the heading should draw to itself. As you move from a main heading to a sub-heading to a sub-sub-heading, your formatting should reflect the lesser importance of each section.

Color

Again, in most academic essays, you should use color sparingly. You don't want your essay to look like a party invitation from the characters of *Rainbow Brite* or *My Little Pony*.

Nevertheless, if you have access to a color printer, it is possible to use color to call attention to important information. As with your use of headings, be consistent and logical in how you apply color to an academic essay.

Using Visuals

As we discussed in Chapter 7, tables, charts, diagrams, photos, maps, and video can all serve as evidence to support your thesis statement. However, an essay—especially one in a first-year writing class—that consists mostly of non-text-based evidence will be seen as an attempt to avoid your responsibilities as a writer.

Professors Susan M. Katz and Lee Odell advise students to "select material (both verbal and visual) that will connect with what you know about your audience's knowledge, values and beliefs about the topic."

Here are a few specific tips as you make final decisions about how to employ your visuals:

- Use brief and accurate captions for each visual.
- Be sure to document the sources of all visuals in your Works Cited page (see Appendix II).
- Don't use more than one or two visuals per page: you don't want to overwhelm your reader.
- Provide white space around visuals.
- Make sure the text commenting on a visual is close to where the visual actually appears.
- Consider cropping images that contain more information than you need. (If you do so, you will want to note that change in the text of your essay.)
- Above all, be certain that each visual is necessary.

Pull Quotes

One of the most common design elements in magazines is the "pull quote": an excerpt from the piece you are reading that is placed in a larger, and sometimes distinctive, typeface. When you turn to a new page, the pull quote is likely the first thing you will read, so much so that it almost has the impact of a visual. Normally, pull quotes are used when a magazine editor wants to highlight a particular point the author is making or to convince the reader that the article itself is worth spending more time on. Adding a pull quote to your essay is as simple as inserting a text box somewhere on the page, and then adding a telling quotation from the surrounding text. As always, though, your instructor should be the ultimate arbiter of whether or not a pull quote enhances an essay or seems merely gimmicky.

WHEN YOU TURN TO A NEW PAGE, THE PULL QUOTE IS LIKELY THE FIRST THING YOU WILL READ.

Seeing the Big Picture

If you have a large screen computer monitor, you can shrink the size of your essay so that most or all of the pages fit onto one screen. It doesn't matter that you can't read individual words; just look at the overall layout. Is this the sort of open, inviting document you would want to read? Or is your essay cramped and forbidding, the kind of document your professor is likely to keep moving to the bottom of a stack of student essays?

If you are working on a laptop with a small screen, you can run the same "big picture" test by printing out all the pages, placing them in numerical order on the floor and stepping back to get an overall visual impression of the essay.

Word Count

Finally, if your instructor gives you a word count range for your essay, try to come as close to that requirement as possible. Make sure you know whether or not your Works Cited page is included as part of the total number of words (it usually isn't). If you have a page rather than a word count, be sure that what you're turning in meets the minimum writing requirements. You don't want it to appear as though you've slacked off on the required writing and filled the space up with pictures instead.

Design and Evaluation Checklist

Remember that design elements that call attention to themselves in an academic essay are like Habañero peppers: one or two go a long way. Therefore, before you begin proofreading your essay, you'll want to answer the following questions:

- Do design and presentation add to the overall readability of your essay?
- Is your design pattern consistent throughout the essay?
- Have you taken into account the fact that this is an academic essay and exercised appropriate restraint in design and presentation?
- If you have departed from a traditional format, is your new format likely to be more persuasive to your audience?

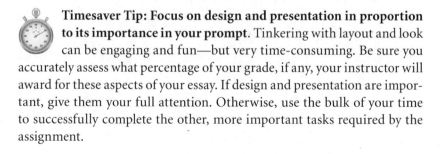 **Timesaver Tip: Focus on design and presentation in proportion to its importance in your prompt.** Tinkering with layout and look can be engaging and fun—but very time-consuming. Be sure you accurately assess what percentage of your grade, if any, your instructor will award for these aspects of your essay. If design and presentation are important, give them your full attention. Otherwise, use the bulk of your time to successfully complete the other, more important tasks required by the assignment.

PROOFREADING

While most professors rightly tell their students not to take a bad grade as a personal judgment, if you turn in careless, sloppy work, your instructor is going to, at least in part, see you as a careless, sloppy person. In that sense, you are your work.

Of course, maybe you *are* a careless, sloppy person, but do you really want to present yourself that way to someone who is awarding you a grade? Proofreading your essay is like making sure you don't have a mustard stain on your clothes when you go out on a date. If that thought doesn't inspire you, think of your essay as a precursor to all the documents you will present to people throughout your adult life: the work on which you will be judged and paid as an adult. Proofreading represents your final opportunity to make sure you shine—or flop.

The first order of business when proofreading is to print out a hard copy. You may be thinking, "But I'm so close to being done, why waste the paper?" The answer is because you nearly always notice previously unseen problems in your writing when you view it in a different medium. And a paper copy—whatever the latest technology may be—is still the best way to get a feel for what you've actually produced.

Once you have a hard copy in front of you, read aloud and slowly, just as you did when editing. If your editing work went well, most of the errors that you heard the last time around will be gone. But it's the rare draft that comes in absolutely perfect. I sometimes bet my own students a dollar that I can find at least one error on the first page of any essay they submit. Although I don't actually collect the money, so far I've never lost the bet.

While the ultimate responsibility is your own, it's always helpful to have someone else give your essay a final proofreading. This is one of those little favors that a fellow student can do for you, which you can return sometime in the near future. Give the person his or her own hard copy to work with and ask for markings in pen or pencil. If the person is physically present when you receive the marked copy, don't hesitate to ask questions—or to challenge a marking if you think it's incorrect.

Proofreading comes at the end of the process, most likely within 24 hours of the time you plan to hand in your essay, so you won't be making big changes at this point. This *is* the time, though, to catch those missing commas and wrong words—the silly mistakes that seem so obvious when you see them marked by your instructor.

There are specific editing and proofreading marks that you can make on an essay in pen or pencil to indicate that you recognize you have made a mistake with your printed draft. However, unless you are sitting in the classroom about to hand in your essay, it is nearly always better to simply correct the mistakes on your digital document and print out a new page.

Timesaver Tip: Don't do a final proofreading until you have completely revised and edited your draft. It's never a bad idea to correct small errors as you see them. However, if you move into the final proofreading process while you still have major changes to make, much of your time will be wasted.

TITLES

For many writers, the time to title an essay is at the very end of the composition process. Just as a master chef waits until a chocolate soufflé is almost ready to be served before sprinkling confectioner's sugar on top, these authors hold off on their title until they know their work is exactly the way they want it.

Of course you may well have thought of a great title even before you began writing. If so, hopefully you wrote it at the top of your essay. In any event, the title is the first thing your reader sees, and while it may not have quite as much impact as your opening sentence, it can serve to interest, or discourage interest, right from the start.

Naturally, you'll want to avoid generic titles like "Essay" and "Essay #1." Yes, these basic labels will help your instructor keep track of which paper you are turning in, but they also reflect a general lack of thought. Titles often forecast the thesis statement, so the more specific you can be, the better.

One of the conventions of naming academic essays is to split the title in two using a colon. The first part of the title draws the reader in with a compelling hook, while the second half is more descriptive and specific. For example: "The Greatest Title Ever: A Study of How to Engage Your Reader with Your Very First Words."

Titles in the Humanities, not surprisingly, tend to be more imaginative than in the sciences and social sciences, sometimes making use of **alliteration**, the repetition of initial sounds in words: "The Three Thrushes of Thurston Drive: One Family's Legacy of Giving Singing Lessons."

In her book *Stylish Academic Writing*, Helen Sword reminds writers that "your title announces your intention to be serious, humorous, detailed, expansive, technical or accessible," and makes the following suggestions for generating a "tempting title":

- Ask a question.
- Set a scene.
- Offer a challenging statement of fact or opinion.
- Invoke a metaphor.

Whatever you decide to title your paper, don't get too cutesy. After all, you are writing an academic essay, not *Sleepless in Seattle*. Professor John Ruszkiewicz says that a bad title—one that is too fanciful or suggestive— "like a silly screen name or email address, will haunt you," and there is no point in being haunted by a title.

A few more title basics:

- The title is centered.
- All the main words in a title are capitalized. Minor words are in lower case.
- Do not use quotation marks around the title (although you do use quotation marks when *referring* to the title of an essay).

 Timesaver Tip: As you compose your essay, write down every title you think of, no matter how unlikely it seems at the time. Then go back later on and sift through your collection of possible titles. If you are using a colon to separate the two parts of your title, you will frequently find that you can mix and match different phrases to create the most effective title.

CAROLINE'S REVISION

Let's look now at one writer's efforts to bring a draft to completion. Below is Caroline Stubbs's revision of "Problems with Facebook," which we first encountered in the previous chapter. Caroline listened to suggestions from me (her instructor), two tutors, her peer writing group, and her mother and brother. Ultimately, though, the revision is a tribute to Caroline's hard work and her smart and savvy decisions about what advice to take—and what to ignore.

Caroline Stubbs
Professor Starkey
English 110
June 12, 2014

"We Have Issues": Problems with Facebook

My current status update in regard to Facebook is a big thumbs down. In a *Time* magazine article entitled "Gen-M: A Dad's Encounter with the Vortex of Facebook," Michael Duffy worries about the way many teens seem to have an illusion of privacy on the site. He also has concerns about Facebook's "darker passages," such as "defamatory speech." I agree with Duffy that young people don't fully consider their actions on Facebook, and I'm very concerned with three main issues: lack of privacy, loss of productivity (wasting time), and the prevalence of stalking and cyberbullying. Because of these overall negative effects, people, especially those in my generation, should begin migrating away from their Facebook pages as soon as possible.

Issue 1: Privacy

In his article on being the parent of a "wired" teen, Michael Duffy points out that teens seem to "think their lives are private" on Facebook, "as long as their parents aren't tuning in." This is a real problem. In high school, I had friends who posted pictures of themselves at parties drunk all the time, and the consequences were real. Our soccer coach, for example, heard rumors that we were drinking and there is a zero tolerance policy for drinking on the team. If a player is caught with alcohol, she is automatically off the team. My senior year, one player, who didn't get much field time, showed the coach a Facebook picture of other players partying. At that point, our coach had to follow through, even if he didn't want to. Three of our best players got kicked off the team, which meant we lost in the first round of our regional playoffs. When I asked my friends what they were thinking when they posted those pictures, they just said, "We never thought an adult would see them!"

My experience with this self-denial toward Facebook is common. In her book *Cyberbullying: What Counselors Need to Know*, Professor Sheri Bauman recounts a meeting with a group of high school students. She asked if any of them had posted something on their Facebook or MySpace pages that they wouldn't want their mothers to see. They all said they had. Then Bauman asked them if they knew that college admissions officers and employers often screen candidates by looking at these pages for inappropriate content. Once again, all the students were aware of this, but they didn't think anything bad would happen to them. Bauman asked the students, "'Isn't that what girls say about getting pregnant when they have sex without protection?' and they all laughed and said, 'Exactly!' So, at some level they understood the absence of logic in their thinking, but their adolescent sense of invincibility apparently prevailed" (77). My friends on the soccer team were the same way. The adult side of their brain told them they should worry about their privacy, but the teenager side told them it was uncool to care.

Issue 2: Productivity

Michael Duffy says he's most upset about time-wasting on Facebook. He even calls Facebook a "time vortex." Granted, even someone like John C. Dvorak, one of the early advocates of the Internet, complains that "the opportunity for these machines [our personal computers] to steal time is phenomenal." And it's not just workers who are losing their precious time. According to a study done by Ohio State University, "college students who use Facebook spend less time studying and have lower grades than students who don't use the popular social networking site" (Gaudin).

COLLEGE STUDENTS WHO USE FACEBOOK SPEND LESS TIME STUDYING AND HAVE LOWER GRADES THAN STUDENTS WHO DON'T USE THE POPULAR SOCIAL NETWORKING SITE.

It's true that not all time spent on Facebook is wasted. I might take an hour to write a long message to my father who lives across the country, and that is time well spent. Keeping up with friends I don't see is also, in my view, time well spent. However, I agree that a lot of people are wasting a lot of time that could be spent studying, exercising, or just talking to real live people. A 2012 study cited by Marcia Clemmitt in *CQ Researcher* indicates "Nine in 10 Americans ages 13 to 17 use Facebook." That is a very worrying statistic.

Issue 3: Stalking and Cyberbullying

The "dark side" of Facebook concerns me the most. Facebook presents an ideal environment for bullies and stalkers. Teens with no impulse control can write things that are cruel and hurtful on Facebook and then somehow feel more anonymous when they do it. As attorney Cal Rose points out, "the Internet insulates cyberbullies from their victims, which prevents aggressors from directly observing the effects of their words and actions." These bullies can spread hateful rumors that are so difficult to overcome, especially when they are in print.

Facebook is also an ideal place for stalkers to operate. In fact, a study called "College Students' Facebook Stalking of Ex-Partners" published in the journal *Cyberpsychology, Behavior and Social Networking* shows that cyberbullying and stalking are related: "As today's youths...age and begin dating, they may be more willing to use the same behaviors, which may cross over to COP [Cyber Obsessional Pursuit] and cyberstalking" (Lyndon, Bonds-Raacke, Cratty 715). Though we have laws against someone physically stalking you, it's hard to monitor what another person does online. After I broke up with my high school boyfriend, he sent endless messages to my Facebook account. When I blocked him, he started doing the same to my friends. He would even create "fake" accounts and try to friend request me. It was never ending! I started using Facebook less and Snapchat more, which is a fairly common transition for people these days. Facebook needs to take some responsibility for this problem because it is providing a forum for individuals who are mentally unstable with a bad (sometimes violent) intent toward someone else.

Of course my story is nothing compared to Rebecca Sedwick's. To look at the Facebook profile photograph of Rebecca, you would think she was any other 12-year-old girl: carelessly brushed brown hair, brown eyes, shy, maybe a little mischievous, probably a lot of fun. However, Rebecca was bullied relentlessly on Facebook for months. When she could no longer take it, she climbed to the top of an abandoned industrial plant and jumped off. To me, the saddest thing is that the two girls who did the most bullying didn't even care. One girl even posted the following comment on Facebook about Rebecca's death: "Yes IK I bullied REBECCA nd she killed herself but IDGAF" (Alvarez). (Of course IDGAF stands for "I don't give a f---.") This girl and her friend were arrested, but they were soon released because there are no real laws against bullying.

Maybe *some* stalkers and cyberbullies would stop if they could actually *see* the harm they were causing, but the case of Rebecca Sedwick shows that, even at a young age some people seem to be pure evil. And if we think these Facebook bullies will grow up and out of tormenting their fellow human beings, we should think again. In their article "An Exploratory Study of Cyberbullying with Undergraduate University Students," researchers Carol Walker, Beth Rajan Sockman and Steven Koehn "found a significant positive correlation between being a bully in university, high school and elementary school" (31). Even more worrying, Facebook was listed as the single most used technology when it comes to cyberbullying (35). Unfortunately, as Rebecca's case demonstrates, there isn't much we can do, even in the court system—and forget about at school. Legal expert Thomas Wheeler writes in "Facebook Fatalities: Students, Social Networking, and the First Amendment," "Because these attacks take place in the cyberworld, the traditional pupil disciplinary framework is ill-suited to deal with this behavior" (183).

Conclusion: G2G Facebook

Granted, Facebook is a useful tool for bringing people together, and it's not all bad. However, issues like those I have raised about privacy, productivity, stalking and cyberbullying show that the bad outweighs the good. As I mentioned earlier, young people are beginning to leave Facebook, as suggested in *Time* magazine: "New research shows that Generation Z favors anonymous or self-destructing social media over more permanent and identifiable identities on Facebook or Twitter, and they're voting with their feet; some studies estimate that over 11 million young people have left Facebook since 2011" (Alter). My suggestion is this: if you are one of the lucky few who don't have a Facebook page, don't get one. And if you are already on Facebook, start weaning yourself off of it. If you log on ten times a day, cut it down to five, then two, then one, then every other day, and once a week until you feel comfortable announcing to your friends that you are closing your account because you have been "cured" of your issues with this social network. As for me, I'm unfriending Facebook today.

Works Cited

Alter, Charlotte. "Oversharenting Victims Rebel: The Quest for Online Anonymity." *Time*, 21 Jan. 2013, time.com/2018/oversharenting -victims-rebel-the-quest-for-online-anonymity. Accessed 30 May 2014.

Alvarez, Lizette. "Felony Counts for 2 in Suicide of Bullied 12-Year Old." *New York Times*, 15 Oct. 2013, nyti.ms/1E0NkP7. Accessed 2 June 2014.

Bauman, Sheri. *Cyberbullying: What Counselors Need to Know.* American Counseling Association, 2010.

Clemmitt, Marcia. "Social Media Explosion." *The CQ Researcher*, vol. 23, no. 4, 2013, library.cqpress.com/cqresearcher/document.php?id =cqresrre2013012500. Accessed 5 June 2014.

Duffy, Michael. "Gen-M: A Dad's Encounter with the Vortex of Face- book." *Time*, 19 Mar. 2006, content.time.com/time/subscriber /article/0,33009,1174704,00.html. Accessed 22 May 2014.

Dvorak, John C. "Lost Productivity Lament." *PC Magazine* 28.11 (2009): 1. *Academic Search Premier*, libproxy.sbcc.edu:2048/login?url=https: //search.ebscohost.com/login.aspx?direct=true&db=aph&AN=47158826 &site=ehost-live&scope=site. Accessed 10 June 2014.

Gaudin, Sharon. "Study: Facebook Users Get Lower Grades in College." *Computerworld.com*, 13 Apr. 2009, www.computerworld.com /article/2524252/web-apps/study--facebook-users-get-lower-grades -in-college.html. Accessed 8 June 2014.

Lyndon, Amy, Jennifer Bonds-Raacke, and Alyssa D. Cratty. "College Stu- dents' Facebook Stalking of Ex-Partners." *Cyberpsychology, Behavior & Social Networking*, vol. 14, no. 12, 2011, pp. 711–16. *Academic Search Premier*, doi: 10.1089/cyber.2010.0588. 7 June 2014.

"Rebecca's Stand Against Bullying." *Facebook*, n.d., www.facebook.com /rebeccasstand. Accessed 2 June 2014.

Rose, S. Cal. "From LOL to Three Months in Jail: Examining the Validity and Constitutional Boundaries of the Arkansas Cyberbullying Act Of

2011." *Arkansas Law Review*, vol. 65, no. 4, 2012, pp. 1001–29. *Academic Search Premier*, libproxy.sbcc.edu:2048/login?url=https://search.ebscohost .com/login.aspx?direct=true&db=aph&AN=84949987&site=ehost -live&scope=site. Accessed 2 June 2014.

"Symbol Thumbs Down." *Wikimedia Commons*, 20 March 2006, commons .wikimedia.org/wiki/File:Symbol_thumbs_down.svg. Accessed 30 May 2014.

Walker, Carol M., Beth Rajan Sockman, and Steven Koehn. "An Exploratory Study of Cyberbullying With Undergraduate University Students." *Techtrends: Linking Research & Practice to Improve Learning*, vol. 55, no. 2, 2011, pp. 31–38. *Academic Search Premier*, doi: 10.1007/ s11528-011-0481-0. Accessed 1 June 2014.

Wheeler, Thomas. "Facebook Fatalities: Students, Social Networking, and the First Amendment." *Pace Law Review*, vol. 31, no. 1, 2011, pp. 182–227. *Academic Search Premier*, libproxy.sbcc.edu:2048/login?url=https: //search.ebscohost.com/login.aspx?direct=true&db=aph&AN=60797301 &site=ehost-live&scope=site. Accessed 29 May 2014.

A Strong Revision

If you go back and read Caroline's first draft in Chapter 9, you'll see what an enormous amount of progress she's made. Of course she didn't get from that draft to this one in a single step: two other drafts, and many hours of conferencing and revising separate her start from her finish. Among the many improvements Caroline made to her first draft are the following:

Title

Caroline has turned her original title "Problems with Facebook" into her subtitle, and added a catchy main title, which puns on the word "issues."

Introduction

Caroline uses the Facebook terms "status update" and "thumbs down" to draw us into the essay, and then quotes from, and identifies, the *Time* magazine article that inspired some of her ideas.

Thesis

Caroline retains the main focus of her original thesis, but she reframes it so that it is more specific and arguable.

Organization

After conducting research on each of her main points, Caroline concluded that her weakest section was the one on productivity, so she sandwiched it between her two stronger topics, ending with the most detailed section, on stalking and cyberbullying.

Research

The essay's level of research is vastly improved. Caroline has cited 11 secondary sources: four academic journals, two long-established national magazines, the *New York Times* newspaper, two reputable websites, and a book on cyberbullying. While she cites *Time* magazine twice, there are no other repeated sources, which shows she has researched widely and avoided the lazy practice of taking numerous quotations from just a few sources. She may have gone a bit overboard on her research, but every time Caroline makes a claim, she backs it up with evidence from a reliable source.

Headings

Each main section is called out in bold headings, with each section's focus named and numbered. Caroline cleverly refers back to her title by using the word "Issue" in each heading.

Layout and Visuals

The essay contains one digital image (free from Wikimedia Commons) and one pull quote to offset the sometimes dense text. Caroline had also wanted to use Rebecca Sedwick's Facebook photo, but the image is owned by her family, and out of respect to Rebecca's memory, Caroline decided not to "poach" the photograph, settling for a written description instead.

Conclusion

Caroline combines several different techniques from the section on conclusions. She includes a quotation from an expert, and then she once again uses Facebook terminology in her section heading ("G2G") and her closing sentence ("unfriend").

Documentation

Caroline has cited all her sources, introducing most of them with a signal phrase that includes the author's name and occupation and the title of the piece. These internal citations are also correctly documented on a Works Cited page (see Appendix II for details).

KNOWING WHEN TO STOP

"A poem is never finished," the French poet Paul Valéry famously proclaimed, "it is only abandoned." You are writing essays, of course, not poems, and you probably don't want to "abandon" your essay, but Valéry was on to something nevertheless.

In a very different area of human endeavor, Mike Scioscia, manager of the Los Angeles Angels, tells his players to "fight that tendency to say, 'This is a big game, and I'm going to hit a ball 430 feet,' when you're only capable of hitting one 410 feet. That will lead to a negative result 100 out of 100 times."

You might be wondering if a poet and a baseball manager are really the best authorities to quote in the final section of the final chapter of this book, but I would argue that these experts on "serious play" and "knowing when to stop" are the perfect "valedictorians" for saying farewell. At any point in your writing career, you are capable of "hitting the ball" just so far. No worries. And no piece of writing is ever as perfect as you might want it to be. That's okay.

Therefore, write to your strengths, and know when you've done your best. Turn in your essay when it's due, and then exhale: there is a time and place to let everything go.

Timesaver Tip: Celebrate! You've finished writing your essay—congratulations! Take some time off to savor your achievement. Successfully completing a task is the ultimate timesaver because the next time you face a similar project, you'll have more confidence and a better sense of how to accomplish what you need to do quickly and efficiently.

Questions and Suggestions FOR You

1. Print out a copy of your draft and place the pages on the floor. Where can you add visuals to enhance your argument? What can you do to accentuate the essay's organization and readability?
2. Draw up a list of titles and use the best one.
3. Print out a draft of your essay and proofread it. Make the corrections,

and then print out another draft and let someone you trust give the essay another proofreading.

Questions and Suggestions FROM You

List three questions you still have after reading this section. Start by review-ing the chapter. If that method doesn't inspire three questions, think about the overall topic of preparing to turn in your final draft. What don't you know about the subject that you would still like to know?

1. _____

_____

_____

_____

2. _____

_____

_____

_____

3. _____

_____

_____

_____

Describe one activity related to "handing it over" *not mentioned in this chap-ter* that you think would be helpful to do in class. Any successful activity in any course you've ever taken might serve as a model.

_____

_____

_____

_____

_____

Genres of Academic Writing

ANALYZING A TEXT
ARGUING A POSITION
PROPOSING A SOLUTION
MAKING AN EVALUATION

We briefly discussed "genre" in Chapter 2, when we learned that, at least for our purposes, the word means "a category of writing." While scholars who study writing now include everything from narrative poetry to direct mail advertisements as "genres" of writing, your professor will likely be thinking of the word in fairly traditional terms.

The four sample essays in this appendix cover the four most frequently assigned genres of college writing: analysis, argument, proposals, and evaluation. Each genre has a fairly clear set of expectations for both writers and readers. Those expectations are described below, with a student essay to illustrate the genre.

Of course, academic writing very often combines genres. As you analyze a text you may also be arguing a position. When you propose a solution, it's very likely that you'll also be making a number of evaluations. Unless your instructor indicates otherwise, I strongly recommend that you allow these genres to blend naturally and in the most effective way possible. Think of each genre as one of several possible strategies for persuading your reader to buy into your argument.

ANALYZING A TEXT

Analysis is the core of academic writing. When you analyze something, you take it apart, look it over, and see how it works. You "break it down," to use the common phrase. As you move through your undergraduate career, you may be required to analyze everything from a novel to a painting to a computer program. However, whatever you are assigned to examine, you will always need to begin by looking closely, again and again. That means when the object of your analysis is a written text, you will have to read it multiple times, taking notes and making sure you comprehend every word.

As you come to understand a text, you will begin to have an opinion of it. The text works, or doesn't work, because of certain things the author is doing with language. The text is your evidence, so you should quote it the way you would any other source: accurately and judiciously. In other words, make sure you say what the author has actually said—and don't quote more (or less) than is necessary to prove your point.

It helps, of course, to have the vocabulary to discuss your subject. If you're analyzing a poem, you'll want to be able to use terms like "enjambment" and "alliteration" and "caesura." If you're breaking down a painting, words like "perspective" and "scumble" and "dead coloring" will be useful. And if you're coding software, you'll want to be familiar with "Java native language" and "floating points" and "underflow."

That said, if you don't have the technical vocabulary of a specialized field, you can still usually make intelligent observations and describe what you see as precisely as possible.

The following essay by Jeremy Hill, for instance, was assigned in a first-year writing class. As the prompt shows, the instructor did not expect the students to have any historical background or to have any specialized knowledge of rhetorical terms like "exordium," "parallelism," or "hyperbole." Nevertheless, Jeremy was able to write a convincing analysis of the speech simply by reading it carefully and then separating it into what he saw as its main component parts. His essay meets all of the criteria of a strong textual analysis because it

- begins with a brief description of the subject,
- breaks the subject down into smaller parts,
- relies primarily on the text itself for evidence,
- uses frequent short quotations as evidence, and
- concludes with an overall appreciation of the subject.

What follows is an edited version of Jeremy's essay, originally written in class. (Because it was an in-class assignment, this essay, unlike the others, includes no research.)

Here is the text Jeremy was analyzing:

Queen Elizabeth's Speech to Her Troops at Tilbury
August 9, 1588

My loving people,

We have been persuaded by some that are careful of our safety, to take heed how we commit ourselves to armed multitudes, for fear of treachery; but I assure you I do not desire to live to distrust my faithful and loving people. Let tyrants fear, I have always so behaved myself that, under God, I have placed my chiefest strength and safeguard in the loyal hearts and good-will of my subjects; and therefore I am come amongst you, as you see, at this time, not for my recreation and disport,* but being resolved, in the midst and heat of the battle, to live and die amongst you all; to lay down for my God, and for my kingdom, and my people, my honour and my blood, even in the dust.

I know I have the body but of a weak and feeble woman; but I have the heart and stomach of a king, and of a king of England too, and think foul scorn that Parma or Spain, or any prince of Europe, should dare to invade the borders of my realm; to which rather than any dishonour shall grow by me, I myself will take up arms, I myself will be your general, judge, and rewarder of every one of your virtues in the field.

I know already, for your forwardness you have deserved rewards and crowns; and We do assure you in the word of a prince, they shall be duly paid you. In the mean time, my lieutenant general shall be in my stead, than whom never prince commanded a more noble or worthy subject; not doubting but by your obedience to my general, by your concord in the camp, and your valour in the field, we shall shortly have a famous victory over those enemies of my God, of my kingdom, and of my people.

*disport = diversion, entertainment

And here is the instructor's prompt:

Queen Elizabeth's speech was given in the port town of Tilbury not long after the English repelled the Spanish Armada in the Battle of Gravelines, but before they knew they had won the war. However, I don't want you to be concerned about the specific historical circumstances that prompted Elizabeth to come to Tilbury. Instead, keep your focus on the speech itself and write a short essay that identifies and discusses the strategies Elizabeth uses to motivate her troops.

Them's Fightin' Words!
An Analysis of Queen Elizabeth's Speech
to Her Troops at Tilbury
by
Jeremy Hill

You might not expect the Queen of England to come across as a tough guy, but that's exactly what happens in "Queen Elizabeth's Speech to Her Troops at Tilbury." Walter White has nothing on Elizabeth as she motivates her soldiers to keep fighting against the Spanish Armada. Elizabeth uses four main strategies to get her troops back into battle: she plays on their loyalty, she backs up her words with deeds, she appeals to their greed, and she takes advantage of the fact that she is a woman rather than a man.

Elizabeth plays on her troops' loyalty to England and the Queen, insisting that because she has been a good ruler, her soldiers should be faithful subjects. She begins her speech by calling her troops "My loving people." She says that while some of her advisors have tried to convince her not to come to the battlefield "for fear of treachery," she isn't afraid because she knows they are her "faithful and loving people." Repeating the phrase "loving people" emphasizes the proper role of a Queen's subjects. She drives the point home by saying that while "tyrants" might fear their subject, a good ruler like her can always rely on "the loyal hearts and good-will" of her people. Elizabeth winds up her speech by repeating this theme of mutual loyalty. She has no doubt of their "obedience," and she says their fortunes are joined, ending with a rallying cry, "we shall shortly have a famous victory over those enemies of my God, of my kingdom, and of my people." Essentially, Elizabeth is suggesting we all win, or we all lose together.

Of course, actions speak louder than words, and Elizabeth backs up her words by actually being there on the battlefield among her troops. It's easy to imagine that she could have sent someone else to make this speech, like the "lieutenant general" she mentions in the last paragraph. However, she is out in there on the front lines, even though the enemy could be nearby. The "armed multitudes" she mentions in the first paragraph could be referring to the Spanish, or it could even be referring to her own army. Either way, she shows her bravery by risking death and appearing to her troops in person.

Elizabeth not only expresses lofty ideals, she also speaks to more earthly concerns, like her soldiers' greed. At the end of the second paragraph, she says she will be her soldiers' general and judge, but also "the rewarder of every one of your virtues in the field." She implies that each battle they win, each person they kill, will result in financial reward. In the very next sentence, she emphasizes the monetary aspect of fighting: "I know already, for your forwardness you have deserved rewards and crowns; and We do assure you in the word of a prince, they shall be duly paid you." Bouncing back and forth between God and virtue to battlefield spoils might seem inappropriate to some, but Elizabeth shows her awareness of the actual conditions on the ground and the type of people who are defending England.

Elizabeth's strongest argument, though, comes by reversing gender roles. Her soldiers might think, "Why should we fight and potentially die for a *woman*?" But she plays on that seeming weakness by demonstrating how tough she is, which by implication means that her male soldiers should be even tougher. Elizabeth ends her first paragraph by declaring she is "resolved, in the midst and heat of the battle, to live and die amongst you all; to lay down for my God, and for my kingdom, and my people, my honour and my blood, even in the dust." That's a pretty big claim! She goes on to admit that even though she is "a weak and feeble woman" she still has "the heart and stomach of a king, and of a king of England too." Elizabeth was the daughter of Henry the Eighth, another monarch with a big heart (and an even bigger stomach!).

When first reading "Queen Elizabeth's Speech to Her Troops at Tilbury," you might be surprised that she manages to convey so much passion in so few words. However, I think the longer a speech is, the less effective it is. Lincoln's Gettysburg Address is another good example of a short speech that has had a big impact. The most important qualities in a speech are saying what you need to say clearly and passionately. After that, you should get off the stage and let your words take effect, and that's exactly what Queen Elizabeth does.

ARGUING A POSITION

Professors across disciplines will often ask you to take a position on a topic. Do you agree with one side or the other? Why or why not? What evidence can you marshal to support your opinion?

Especially if you are taking a class outside your major, you may frequently have no opinion on the topic at all. Or your only opinion may be, "Who cares?" Addressing that dilemma is important. In fact, learning to care about something you'd previously considered unimportant is one of the most valuable skills you can learn at university.

It's boring to write about a topic that everyone agrees on, so your instructor will generally ask you to tackle something controversial. Sometimes this can be local, a campus issue, say, like housing, security, parking, smoking, plagiarism, and so on. Other times your professor will want you to take a look at the wider world.

Each of these subject areas has its negatives and positives. Local issues are, obviously, close to home. You can interview the relevant people, and observe first-hand what's at stake. On the other hand, sometimes those issues may seem trivial. Do you really care if your school colors are green and blue, or green and orange?

National and global issues, by contrast, have much more potential long-range impact on your life. And there is probably a great deal of material you can draw on for your research. However, the more distant the topic, the less connection you may feel to it personally.

Whatever issue you end up arguing for or against, you will need to reaffirm its importance to your readers so that they won't think, "Who cares?" Providing background information will be necessary, even if the subject is close to your readers' hearts. And of course the information you choose to focus on will help frame the debate, allowing you to nudge your readers in the direction you want them to go right from the start. As always, concrete and specific evidence will carry more weight than vague generalities.

Finally, when arguing a position, it's important that you maintain the tone of someone who is sensible and reliable. The more heated the topic, the more you'll want to sound like the voice of reason amid a welter of impassioned, and possibly irrational, opinions.

Emma Sandrolini's prompt was to research a controversial current topic and take a strong stand in favor of one side or the other. Emma has done exactly that, arguing in her essay "Challenges for Women's Education in Afghanistan" (written in the autumn of 2013) that the Taliban's trampling of women's rights has been facilitated by the duplicity of Afghan president Hamid Karzai and the withdrawal of American troops. Emma's essay

- offers an opinion on a matter of public concern,
- doesn't shy away from controversy,
- reaffirms the importance of the issue,
- provides background information,
- uses concrete evidence to support the claim, and
- maintains an authoritative tone.

🚫 **Avoid This Common Error: Writing an argument essay that refuses to take sides**. If you don't have strong feelings on a topic, you may be tempted to write an essay that tries to give equal credence to both sides. That's an admirable goal, but if you don't ultimately come down in favor of one side or another, you'll just end up looking wishy-washy, as though you hadn't taken the trouble to make up your mind.

Challenges for Women's Education in Afghanistan
by
Emma Sandrolini

According to a June 2011 global survey cited by Jennifer Heath in her book *Land of the Unconquerable: The Lives of Contemporary Afghan Women*, Afghanistan was the "world's most dangerous country in which to be born a woman" (13). Discrimination has plagued women in Afghanistan for over three decades, but conditions sank to a new low when the Taliban came to power in 1996. According to the Revolutionary Association of Women of Afghanistan (RAWA), the country has the highest mortality rate and the lowest literacy rate among women in the world. The extremist government has continually violated Afghan women's rights, in particular their right to an education. Article 26 of the United Nations' Declaration of Human Rights states, "everyone has the right to education. Education shall be free, at least in the elementary and fundamental stages. Elementary education shall be compulsory" (UDHR). Article 26 also insists that education should "promote understanding, tolerance and friendship among all nations, racial or religious groups, and shall further the activities of the United Nations for the maintenance of peace." Though literacy rates and attendance in school have improved since the fall of the Taliban, the situation for girls and women remains deplorable and far from the goals of Article 26. Ultimately, it is President Hamid Karzai's involvement with the Taliban and the withdrawal of United States troops that have allowed the reassertion of extremist, religious fundamentalist groups who pose a threat to Afghan women's education and general well-being.

To understand the complexity of the issue, we must look back at the history of Afghanistan's government to see *why* it is so difficult and dangerous for Afghan women to get an education. Jennifer Heath notes, "The 1979 Soviet invasion of Afghanistan triggered and intensified a fierce ideological competition among the various Afghan Mujahedin groups. In response...there evolved a local brand of Islamic fundamentalism fueled by the Mujahedin's zeal for fighting a jihad to defeat and expel the communist soviets" (13). Consequently, women's rights took a hit, particularly attitudes toward their education. The once relatively liberal Afghanistan changed to an ultra-conservative society based on indigenous tribal codes, Islamic law and highly orthodox Islamic ideologies (Heath 13).

The Taliban came fully into play in 1989 after the pullout of Soviet forces from Afghanistan. They officially took over in 1996. Their goal was to "create the only 'pure' Islamic state in the world" (Heath 7). To achieve this "pure" state, the Taliban banned television, and movies. However, their most controversial ideology was that women were inferior to men in every way. The Taliban regime "sunk the Afghan education system to a new low, unlike anything seen elsewhere in the modern world, wherein girls were prohibited from attending schools, and female teachers were sent home" (Heath 13). The Taliban policy of keeping girls out of school was based on a very strong cultural prohibition against having women mix with men who were not relatives. According to *Time* magazine reporters Aryn Baker and Ali Safi, those who tried to go against this ruling risked serious harm and even death (41). Fortunately, the United States removed the Taliban from power after the attacks on September 11, 2001.

During Afghanistan's reconstruction, the number of women and girls in school has improved somewhat. As Shireen Khan Burki notes in "The Politics of *Zan* from Amanullah to Karzai," after the fall of the Taliban, initially "the government of the Islamic Republic of Afghanistan took major steps to restore the dignity of its female populace and improve their quality of life" (55). However, the future for women gaining an education once again looks bleak. Laura Kavazanjian thoroughly investigates the issue in her article "Addressing Gender Disparities: An Investigation of Nonformal Education in Afghanistan." Kavazanjian found that in 2010, only 20 percent of girls in Afghanistan were enrolled in primary school and only 12 percent of Afghan women are literate (40). Also, "42 percent of households claim that enrolling girls in primary education 'would be contrary to family commitment, the child's marriage or their tradition'" (Kavazanjian 43). According to Baker and Safi, "More than six years since the fall of the Taliban, fewer than 30% of eligible girls are enrolled in schools, and the infrastructure is so poor that only a tiny fraction are likely to get the education they need to enjoy the fruits of emancipation" (40).

Women are more susceptible to these threats because the Taliban is still *indirectly* involved through President Karzai's rule. According to a Human Rights Watch report, in March of 2012 the Council, Afghanistan's highest Islamic authority, released an edict with a strong Taliban sentiment, which Karzai endorsed, stating, "'Men are fundamental and women are secondary,'" adding that women should avoid "'mingling with strange men in various social activities such as education, in bazaars, in offices and other aspects of life'" ("World Report 2013"). The edict is in sharp contrast to Karzai's rhetoric at the start of his term in office. Karzai's primary goal at this point is to bring peace to Afghanistan. However, it seems as though he is turning to extremist groups, such as the Taliban, to make this happen.

The resurgence of the Taliban is not only due to Afghanistan's government, but also the withdrawal of NATO forces. Though it is not yet finalized that all U.S. forces will be removed from Afghanistan, this withdrawal will present a risk to the stability of Afghanistan. The total elimination of NATO would mean that Afghanistan would no longer receive aid from the United States, and for a country that cannot support itself, this could create an uproar. The withdrawal will also force European countries to pull out and give a yet another boost to the Taliban ("World Report 2013"). Afghanistan and the United States have had their differences, to say the least, but the United States' goal has been bringing stability to Afghanistan. Since 2002, The United States has given 100 billion dollars to Afghanistan for reconstruction ("World Report 2013"), and most of these funds went towards health and education.

Ironically, Afghanistan wouldn't have to rely on extreme Islamic groups or the United States for their stability if women were educated: "Every social and economic index shows that countries with a higher percentage of women with a high school education also have better overall health, a more functional democracy and increased economic performance [and] educated women are a strong bulwark against the extremism that still plagues Afghanistan" (Baker and Safi 41). According to Burki, "Countries that limit women's educational and employment opportunities and their political voice get stuck in a downward spiral. They are poorer, more fragile, have higher levels of corruption, and are more prone to extremism" (58). Female education can also support a developing country like Afghanistan because girls' education lowers birth rates, which improves per capita income. The education of girls and women also boosts agricultural productivity and improves long-term economic growth rates (Burki 58). Though there is no single answer to solve Afghanistan's plight, the education of women is a start in the right direction. If a whole population has the resources to be intelligent and empowered, then the country will follow in that direction.

Unfortunately, complete security in Afghanistan, which is necessary for an effective education system, cannot be achieved until the government cuts ties with extremist groups. If Afghanistan's primary goal is peace at any cost, then including the Taliban will make it unlikely that women's education will progress. On the other hand, if Afghanistan wants to rise above what President Karzai describes as their "weak" and "ineffective" government (Hakim), traditional religious groups and other forces that oppress women need to be eliminated from Afghanistan's governance. Educated, employed women are the answer to Afghanistan's stability, and for all the strides that women have taken to make this a reality, Afghanistan should move forward to a progressive system, not a government that will most likely be intransigent.

Works Cited

Baker, Aryn, and Ali Safi. "The Girl Gap." *Time*, vol. 171, no. 4, 28 Jan. 2008, pp. 40–43. *Academic Search Premiere*, libproxy.sbcc.edu:2048 /login?url=https://search.ebscohost.com/login.aspx?direct=true&db =aph&AN=28541787&site=ehost-live&scope=site. 18 Oct. 2013.

Burki, Shireen Khan. "The Politics of *Zan* from Amanullah to Karzai." Heath and Zahedi, pp. 45–60.

Hakim, Yalda. "Afghanistan's Hamid Karzai Says Nato Caused 'Great Suffering'" *BBC News*. 10 July 2013, www.bbc.com/news/world-24433433. Accessed 28 Oct. 2013.

Heath, Jennifer. "Introduction." Heath and Zahedi, pp. 1–41.

———, and Ashraf Zahedi, editors. *Land of the Unconquerable: The Lives of Contemporary Afghan Women*, University of California Press, 2011.

Kavazanjian, Laura. "Addressing Gender Disparities: An Investigation of Nonformal Education in Afghanistan." *Women's Policy Journal of Harvard*, vol. 7, 2010, pp. 39–50. *Academic Search Premier*, libproxy.sbcc .edu:2048/login?url=https://search.ebscohost.com/login.aspx?direct =true&db=aph&AN=57236178&site=ehost-live&scope=site. 20 Oct. 2013.

"RAWA Literacy Program for Afghan Women (RAWA Photos)." *Revolutionary Association of the Women of Afghanistan*, Oct. 2004, www.rawa.org/x-courses.htm. 5 Nov. 2013.

"Universal Declaration of Human Rights." *United Nations*, 10. Dec. 1948, ww.un.org/en/universal-declaration-human-rights. 05 Nov. 2013.

"World Report 2013: Afghanistan." *Human Rights Watch*, [2013], www.hrw.org/world-report/2013/country-chapters/afghanistan. 30 Oct. 2013.

PROPOSING A SOLUTION

It's definitely a pain if you drop your non-water-resistant phone in the toilet, but is that really a problem requiring a full-length paper to articulate the solution? Probably not. Bottom line: you let it dry, vacuum it, put it in a bag of rice—and most likely still end up buying a new phone. It's a nuisance, sure, but it's ultimately too trivial a topic for an academic essay.

On the other end of the spectrum, what about war? That's surely a problem, one that humans have faced, and been unable to solve, for as long as the race has existed. Can you solve the problem of war in 1500 words? I don't think so.

Clearly, then, the first step in deciding on a topic for a problem-solution paper is identifying a problem that's compelling enough to be worth solving, but not so wide-ranging and intractable that your essay is doomed to fail. That means narrowing your topic, as we discussed in Chapter 4, from the broad to the narrow.

Inevitably, of course, proposing the solution to a problem will require research. The more you find out about your problem in advance, the easier it will be to identify the possible solutions you feel most comfortable discussing.

Settling on realistic solutions is the next step. Don't make a larger claim than the evidence in your essay warrants. It's better to acknowledge the limitations of your solution—that is, a reader's potential counterarguments—than to exaggerate the solution's likely effectiveness.

You generally want to strike an even balance between describing the problem and offering solutions, although if most readers are likely to agree on the cause of the problem, you will want to focus your discussion on the solution.

Clearly defined social problems often make for compelling problem-solution essays. In Andrea Bottiani's essay, the subject of obesity has been narrowed down to childhood obesity, with three specific solutions for not entirely solving, but at least attempting to "make a dint in the problem," as she puts it.

Andrea's essay, "Childhood Obesity: Three Possible Solutions," meets the criteria we have just described. It

- focuses on a real problem, one capable of at least a partial solution,
- describes specific aspects of the problem in some detail,
- offers concrete and realistic solutions,
- is thoroughly researched and makes effective use of evidence, and
- addresses possible counterarguments.

Childhood Obesity: Three Possible Solutions
by
Andrea Bottiani

Introduction: A Day at the Zoo

I was at the zoo with my younger siblings a few days ago, and I saw one toddler in a stroller with a bag of Cheetos and another with a cup of sugar-filled soda. As shocking as it is, these children, who can hardly walk and have just begun to eat solid food, are already on the road to poor health. Unfortunately, many children in the United States are overweight, and a significant percentage suffer from a clinically diagnosed disease called obesity, which doctors define as having a body mass index of thirty or higher. According to the Obesity Society, "in the past two decades alone, the number of obese children and adolescents has doubled from 7% to 15.3%" ("Childhood"). Because the emotional and physical consequences of childhood obesity are so great, we must seek to make a dint in the problem of this epidemic. With the help of medical professionals and families across the country, we can work toward addressing three major challenges facing obese children: unhealthy diets, a lack of physical activity, and the negative influence of television and advertising.

Problem 1: Unhealthy Diet

Most nutritionists believe the biggest cause of childhood obesity is diet. Many children eat high calorie foods with little nutritional value because they cost less money than healthy, low-calorie foods. The Farm, Nutrition and Bioenergy Act of 2007 states that "lower-income families have a higher risk for obesity than those from higher-income families" ("Farm"). Food that is high in calories and low in nutritional value is readily available at a low price at almost any kind of grocery or convenience store, which makes it appealing to parents with little money. Also, families involved in government sponsored food programs may be exposed to food that does not have high nutritional value ("Childhood"). Inexpensive and unhealthy fast food can be a problem as well. For example, Chicken McNuggets at McDonald's costs around a dollar and are breaded and fried in grease, whereas a package of four organic healthy chicken breasts can cost ten dollars. Parents who work low-income jobs and long hours may not have the money or time to prepare quality, low calorie meals for their children. This leads children to increased snacking on cheap, unhealthy foods, especially when no one is home to supervise.

Solution 1: Healthy Diet

Obviously, the best way to avoid an unhealthy diet is to change to a healthy one, although millions of people who have tried to do this know how difficult it can be. Nevertheless, with their parents' help, children can make strides forward. Dana Cassell and David Gleaves, editors of *The Encyclopedia of Obesity and Eating Disorders*, point out that "color coding of foods to show calorie amounts can be understood by children as young as age five" (91). One recent study in the *Journal of Community Health* suggested government agencies "could address the risk of sugar-sweetened beverage consumption…by reducing the cost of healthy alternatives (e.g., vouchers for fresh fruit and vegetables)." In addition, the New York State Department of Health makes some very specific recommendations for a healthy diet. They tell parents to "buy fewer high-calorie, low-nutrient foods" and "help children understand that sweets and high-fat treats (such as candy, cookies, or cake) are not everyday foods." At the same time, they warn against "labeling foods as 'good' or 'bad'" because "all foods in moderation can be part of a healthy diet." Finally, the Department of Health advises parents to involve "children in planning, shopping, and preparing meals." By doing so, parents help children to understand their own "food preferences, teach children about nutrition, and encourage them to try a wide variety of foods." Granted, some children will resist this conversion to healthy eating, but if parents are reasonable and persistent, they should be able to help their children make a positive change.

Problem 2: Lack of Physical Activity

According to the Health Services for Children Foundation, obese young people admitted to a "lack of physical activity" (4), expressing "frustration and concern over time constraints and the lack of resources and community support that would allow them to sustain healthy behaviors" (8). Children who are not physically active do not burn the calories and energy that they should. And this lack of activity is not just a physical problem; it also has emotional repercussions. Researchers for the *International Journal of Pediatric Obesity* found that "overweight children with high levels of weight and shape concern are particularly at risk of experiencing psychological problems" (Allen 246). Every kid knows (or at least *should* know) how good it feels to go outside and play until you're exhausted. Not being able to get that sort of exercise will obviously have a negative effect on children.

Solution 2: Schools and Communities

Fortunately, the promotion of athletics and physical activity in the school systems can help students who may suffer from being overweight. As Jana Parízková and Andrew Hills note in their book *Childhood Obesity: Prevention and Treatment*, "school nurses, or sports coaches, are well placed to provide innovative and targeted assistance. Further, most schools have a range of physical facilities and equipment on-site" (355). Schools are the focus of children's lives nine months of the year, so it makes sense that they should be central to solving the problem of obesity.

In addition, some cities have been trying to deal with the problem by creating exercise trails near poor communities. In Steve Hymon's article, "On the Trail of Better Health in South L.A.," he describes one of these projects. Health officials opened a trail that offers beautiful views of Los Angeles, and it is free (B3). According to an article in *Obesity, Fitness and Wellness Week*, living an active lifestyle will increase an individual's metabolism, which will increase his ability to lose weight and burn calories and energy. For a child, participation in a physical activity may also increase her social situation and decrease depression.

Problem 3: TV and Advertising

Another significant contributor to the childhood obesity epidemic is the high frequency of television viewing. This activity involves long periods of sitting. The Obesity Society states that the lack of exercise and the increased consumption of food while staring at a screen is one of the leading causes of obesity in adolescents ages 12–17 ("Childhood"). Obsessive participation in sedentary activities can lead to reclusive behaviors such as an unwillingness to go to school and inability to socialize with peers. Staring at the TV (or a video game) also promotes low self-esteem and other emotional problems, which will only increase with obesity. This creates a vicious cycle in the obese child.

The over-consumption of high-calorie snack foods while doing homework and watching television contributes to the childhood obesity epidemic as well. Children are often not hungry but eat anyway out of habit, and eating when an individual is not hungry increases the risk of obesity ("Childhood"). Many ads on TV focus on food, especially unhealthy snacks. For example, according to Stephanie Allmon, a reporter for the *Fort Worth Star-Telegram*, a small, snack-sized bag of Cheetos has nearly 300 calories and 20 grams of fat but contains absolutely no vitamins. This snack does not even fill a person up. Eating snacks like this day after day without doing any physical activity can easily cause weight gain and eventual obesity.

And it's not just at home that children encounter advertising for unhealthy foods. Christian Davenport, a lawyer and writer for the *Washington Post*, says that many public schools provide soda and candy vending machines on campus. The public schools think that they are accommodating young people when in fact they are encouraging obesity in their adolescent students.

Solution 3: Counter-Advertising & Federal Regulations

If children seem to be negatively affected by all the fast food advertisements on TV, schools have found that they can fight back—by using advertisements. According to one study "promotional signage (highlighting or encouraging low-fat snack options) on vending machines significantly increased low-fat snack sales in secondary schools independently of a range of different pricing strategies" (McDermott 261). In other words, if healthy food has catchy advertising, students buy it even if it costs more than junk food.

However, counter-advertising isn't enough. In a study for *Health Matrix* journal, attorney Andrew Harvey argues that there is plenty of evidence that "child-directed food and beverage television advertisements... [are] a contributing factor" to childhood obesity. Harvey thinks that recent "self-regulation by the industry is a good start," but he believes much more needs to be done. Harvey says, "Congress must step in and use its legislative powers to promulgate a law that effectively restricts children-directed television advertisement techniques" (637). We need the law on our side so can we truly begin helping children live healthier lives.

Conclusion: It All Starts with the Parents

One thing all of these solutions have in common is the necessary involvement of the parents. It may sound harsh to blame parents for their children's obesity, but genetics obviously plays a part in the problem, and lack of guidance and encouragement from the parents can be a real roadblock for the children. The first step for parents is taking care of their own health. One study indicates that "reducing the prevalence of parental overweight and obesity would not only help preventing childhood obesity, but would in general lead to an improved health not only of the children, but also of their parents" (Cassell and Gleaves 6). Parents need to do what I have been suggesting in this essay for their children: eat healthy foods, exercise, and resist advertisements that encourage them to binge out on snack and fast foods. It may be hard for both parents and children at first, but the results will be worth it. Healthier parents will lead to healthier children.

Works Cited

Allen, Karina L., et al. "Why Do Some Overweight Children Experience Psychological Problems? The Role of Weight and Shape Concern." *International Journal of Pediatric Obesity*, vol. 1, no. 4, 2006, pp. 239–247. *Academic Search Premier*, doi: 10.1080/17477160600913552. Accessed 12 Apr. 2016.

Allmon, Stephanie. "Vending Machine Versus the Diet." *Fort Worth Star-Telegram*, 29 Aug. 2006, articles.orlandosentinel.com/2006-08-29/news/VENDINGFOOD_1_calories-and-fat-250-calories-280-calories. Accessed 15 Apr. 2016.

Bammann, Karin, et al. "Early Life Course Risk Factors For Childhood Obesity: The IDEFICS Case-Control Study." *Plos ONE* vol. 9, no. 2, 2014, pp. 1–7. *Academic Search Premier*, doi: 10.1371/journal.pone .0086914. Accessed 15 Apr. 2016.

Cassell, Dana K., and David H. Gleaves. *The Encyclopedia of Obesity and Eating Disorders*. 3rd ed. Facts on File, 2006.

"Childhood Overweight." *Obesity Society*, May 2014, www.obesity.org /resources/facts-about-obesity/childhood-overweight. Accessed 16 Apr. 2016.

Davenport, Christian. "Lawmaker Takes on Childhood Obesity." *Washington Post*, 23 Oct. 2003, www.washingtonpost.com/archive /local/2003/10/23/lawmaker-takes-on-child-obesity/4e612f9c-d4e1 -409b-941e-baf1a0a50e74. Accessed 12 Apr. 2016.

"Farm, Nutrition and Bioenergy Act of 2007." *Congressional Record*, 27 July 2007, www.gpo.gov/fdsys/pkg/CREC-2007-07-27/html/CREC -2007-07-27-pt1-PgH8747-2.htm. Accessed 14 Apr. 2016.

Harvey, Andrew. "A Proposal for Congressionally Mandated Federal Regulation of Child-Directed Food and Beverage Television Advertisements to Combat Childhood Obesity." *Health Matrix: Journal of Law-Medicine*, vol. 23, no. 2, 2013, pp. 607–37. *Academic Search Premier*, libproxy.sbcc.edu:2048/login?url=https://search.ebscohost.com/login.aspx?direct=true&db=aph&AN=91839123&site=ehost-live&scope=site. Accessed 16 Apr. 2016.

Hymon, Steve. "On the Trail of Better Health in South L.A." *Los Angeles Times*, 16 Nov. 2003, articles.latimes.com/2003/nov/16/local/me-trail16. Accessed 15 Apr. 2016.

McDermott, Laura, Martine Stead, and Gerard Hastings. "Does Food Promotion Influence Children's Diet? A Review of the Evidence." *Childhood Obesity: Contemporary Issues*, edited by N. Cameron, et al., Taylor & Francis, 2006, pp. 251–66.

Parízková, Jana, and Andrew Hills. *Childhood Obesity: Prevention and Treatment*. CRC Press, 2005.

"Preventing Childhood Obesity: Tips for Parents." *New York State Department of Health*, June 2012, www.health.ny.gov/prevention/nutrition/resources/obparnts.htm. Accessed 15 Apr. 2016.

Watt, Toni, et al. "Sugar, Stress, and the Supplemental Nutrition Assistance Program: Early Childhood Obesity Risks among a Clinic-Based Sample of Low-Income Hispanics." *Journal of Community Health*, vol. 38, no. 3, 2013, pp. 513–20. *Academic Search Premier*, doi: 10.1007/s10900-012-9641-1. Accessed 16 Apr. 2016.

MAKING AN EVALUATION

It's hard to get through the average day without making an evaluation. What should you eat for breakfast? Yogurt is good for you, but this morning you sure feel like bacon and scrambled eggs. Immediately, your evaluation criteria for breakfasts kick in. How important is it for you to be healthy today? Will you be burning off extra calories, or is this one of those days you'll mostly spend sitting down? These thoughts occur very fast, of course, but you *do* go through the process of assessing the value of one quality (nutrition) over another (taste).

Then it's time to dress, get to school or work, decide what to tell your friends about last night's party (and what to tell your parents), and on, and on. Every situation has a new set of standards by which it is judged, and your job is to match the appropriate situation with the appropriate criterion. Making an evaluation in an academic essay simply brings many of these hidden steps to light.

You may be most familiar with the evaluations of experts through music, video game, movie, and television reviews. You turn to these authorities because you want to know whether or not something is worth your time and money, and you expect that they will not only give you a straightforward and honest evaluation, but that they will back it up with evidence, often in the form of descriptions of whatever is being evaluated.

Your evaluative essay will make many of the same moves as those of a professional reviewer. Early in your essay, you will want to set out your evaluation criteria, briefly describe your object, and state your evaluation. Further descriptions and elaborations of the criteria will take place throughout the essay, but it's important for readers to have an understanding up front of what you're talking about and why you feel about it the way you do.

Often, the evaluation of an object has a very specific audience. If, for instance, you are reviewing the latest version of *World of Warcraft* on a website for video-game enthusiasts, you can be pretty sure that you don't have to spell out the basics of participating in a massively multiplayer online role-playing game. On the other hand, if you are evaluating a decades-old photograph for a contemporary general audience, as Eric Martinez does below, you should spend more time providing basic background information. In either case, you will want to connect your evaluation criteria with the object's purpose and audience.

Whether or not you use the personal pronoun "I" in your evaluation, you will necessarily be drawing on your own opinion of the object. Indeed, evaluations that are the most fun to read are often those in which the evaluator's personality is front and center. That said, no evaluation is convincing without evidence. If you are reviewing a film, you will describe key scenes, briefly quote dialogue, discuss the cinematography, and so on. In his essay "What Makes a Great Photograph? Dorothea Lange's 'Migrant Mother,'" Eric not only describes the photograph in some detail, he also draws on the analysis and evaluations of a number of experts. This combination of intense focus on the object along with authoritative support for your opinions is an especially effective technique in an academic essay.

Evaluators frequently compare their object with similar objects that they find inferior or superior. Someone reviewing the new 50 Cent album, for instance, might consider the extent to which his music has been influenced by mentors like Dr. Dre and Eminem. And even if you admire or despise the thing you are evaluating, it's not a bad idea to consider alternative evaluations: if someone were to love a thing you truly hate (or vice versa), what would be that person's criteria for doing so?

You'll find Eric Martinez covers all these bases in "What Makes a Great Photograph? Dorothea Lange's 'Migrant Mother.'" Eric's essay

- describes the object being evaluated,
- describes the evaluation criteria,
- connects the evaluation criteria with the object's purpose and audience,
- supports personal opinion with specific evidence,
- uses comparison to establish the object's value, and
- considers alternative evaluations.

What Makes a Great Photograph?
Dorothea Lange's "Migrant Mother"
by
Eric Martinez

Dorothea Lange, "Migrant Mother," 1936

What makes a great photograph? According to photographer Larissa Olenicoff, "Good photographs put you in a particular moment in time, they tell a story, or they speak to your emotions" (Graham). The most important element of a *great* photograph is that it does all of the above. If the many people who have praised and written about

Dorothea Lange's famous Depression-era photo of a mother and her three children can be trusted, and I think they can, Lange has taken a great photo. "Destitute Pea Pickers in California: Mother of Seven Children," more commonly known as "Migrant Mother," depicts Florence Owens, a careworn woman, looking into the distance. The heads of two of her children rest on her shoulder. They are turned away from the camera. You can just see the face of the grubby infant resting in her lap. This bleak but beautiful photo fills all three of Olenicoff's criteria: it shows a family in a particular moment of time, it implies a story, and it speaks to the viewer's emotions. I would add one further criteria of my own: a great photograph makes us want to take action on behalf of the person or thing being photographed.

One of the reasons Lange's photograph is so famous is because so many people see it as representative of its moment in time: the Great Depression. Professor James C. Curtis tells the story of how "Migrant Mother" was taken: "Late on a cold, rainy afternoon in March 1936, Dorothea Lange spent 10 minutes photographing the wife and children of a migrant pea picker in Nipomo, California. During that brief time, she made five exposures, one of which is now known as 'Migrant Mother' and is acclaimed as a masterpiece of documentary photography" (116). As critic Christopher Benfy points out, this "is one of the best-known of all American photographs," in part because it so clearly evokes the plight of people during the Depression. In fact, teachers like Susan Riley use the photo "as a way for students to analyze visual art as informational text. Students view the photograph and then use visual thinking strategies to analyze the image and relate it to the Great Depression." In other words, "Migrant Mother" is an entry point into the study of American history.

The story implied by "Migrant Mother" is one of hard times and uncertainty. Somehow this family has found itself on the road. The backdrop of the photograph appears to be a canvas tent, so we assume they no longer have a permanent home. The woman may have been beautiful once, and she is still pretty in a fading sort of way, but the crowsfeet coming from her eyes, the wrinkles on her forehead, and the deep grooves in her cheek all suggest a future in which hard times will continue to wear on her. Also, what about her children? Somehow the family has managed to stay together, but what are they going to eat tonight or tomorrow? How is she going to feed her baby? The story doesn't yet have an ending, but probably it's not going to be a happy one.

As we think about the family's fate, it's hard not to feel the emotional tug of "Migrant Mother." Her clothes are ragged, and her children are dirty. She looks incredibly worried, squinting off into the future, but she also looks determined. Her children are relying on her, and even if we have never been in her situation, we can't help but sympathize with her difficulties. As journalist Julia Baird remarks, "Lange's subjects were poor, but also disciplined, hardworking, and upright." I think we sympathize more with people who look like they are doing their best but have been overwhelmed by circumstances they can't control, and that's exactly what "Migrant Mother" portrays.

The fact that Lange's picture has all of the above qualities means "Migrant Mother" is a great photograph. What makes it even more extraordinary is the way it makes us want to help out the woman and her children. John Louis Lucaites and Robert Hariman point out in an article in *Rhetoric Review* that Lange's photograph "allows one to acknowledge paralyzing fear at the same time it triggers an impulse to do something about it" (38). That is where Lange's artistry really comes in. The picture most of us would take if we saw a poor mother and her children would not necessarily inspire anyone to try and help them. But Lange has found the perfect pose of the beautiful but exhausted mother with her three children clinging to her.

The fact that the photograph makes us want to help those less fortunate was no accident on Lange's part. Linda Gordon writes in her book *Dorothea Lange: A Life Beyond Limits* that "Lange's fleeting glance caught something important because her eye was so trained. Then a second part of her photographic discipline took over—a sense of responsibility—to document a condition and seize visual oppor-tunity" (236). According to her biographer, Anne Whiston Spirn, Lange's "work inspired [John] Steinbeck as he conceived and wrote his powerful novel *The Grapes of Wrath....* Filmmaker Pare Lorenz claimed that Lange's images of migrant workers, which appeared in thousands of newspapers, magazines, and Sunday supplements, and Steinbeck's *The Grapes of Wrath* 'did more for these tragic nomads than all the politicians in the country'" (8). Dorothea Lange seemed pleased that the photo helped people out as much as it made her famous. According to Professor Louis Gawthrop, "For Lange, the value of the picture was in the federal government's response. Once again, the power of her photographic eye was able to enhance the lives of a few homeless migrants."

There are thousands of other photos of Depression-era families that don't have the impact of "Migrant Mother." In fact, Dorothea Lange took four of them herself of Florence Owens and her children. All four of these photographs are shot from further away, and none of them have the same force as the close-up, almost claustrophobic shot we call "Migrant Mother." Granted, not everyone is crazy about the photograph. Michael Zhang points out that Owens's thumb was originally shown "wrapped around the tent pole," but Lange subsequently used the tools of the day to erase this slight blemish. But that's ridiculous nit-picking. "Migrant Mother" has stood the test of time for almost eight decades now, and it is sure to be regarded with veneration for many decades to come.

Works Cited

Baird, Julia. "Seeing Dignity in Poverty." *Newsweek*, vol. 154, no. 20, 16 Nov. 2009, p. 30. *Academic Search Premier*, libproxy.sbcc.edu:2048 /login?url=https://search.ebscohost.com/login.aspx?direct=true&db =aph&AN=45137533&site=ehost-live&scope=site. Accessed 5 Feb. 2017.

Benfey, Christopher. "The Hunger Artists." *New Republic* vol. 240, no 22, 2 Dec. 2009, pp. 44–47. *Academic Search Premier*, libproxy.sbcc.edu:2048 /login?url=https://search.ebscohost.com/login.aspx?direct=true&db =aph&AN=45179697&site=ehost-live&scope=site. Accessed 5 Feb. 2017.

Curtis, James C. "Review of Kartin Beck Ohrn's *Dorothea Lange and the Documentary Tradition*." *Winterthur Portfolio*, vol.18, no. 1, 1983, pp. 116–17.

Gawthrop, Louis C. "Dorothea Lange and Visionary Change." *Society*, vol. 30, no. 5, 1993, pp. 64–67. *Academic Search Premier*, libproxy.sbcc.edu:2048 /login?url=https://search.ebscohost.com/login.aspx?direct=true&db =aph&AN=9308317689&site=ehost-live&scope=site. Accessed 10 Feb. 2017.

Gordon, Linda. *Dorothea Lange: A Life Beyond Limits*. Norton, 2010.

Graham, Ed. "Top Photographers Answer, 'What Makes a Good Photograph?'" *Go See Write*, 8 July 2013, www.goseewrite.com/2013/07/top -photographers-answer-what-makes-a-good-photograph/. Accessed 2 Feb. 2017.

Lange, Dorothea. *Destitute Pea Pickers in California: Mother of Seven Children*, also known as *Migrant Mother*. 1936. National Archives, Washington, DC. *National Archives*, catalog.archives.gov/id/19626. Accessed 2 Feb. 2017.

Lucaites, John Louis, and Robert Hariman. "Visual Rhetoric, Photojournalism, and Democratic Public Culture." *Rhetoric Review*, vol. 20, no. 1–2, 2001, pp. 37–42.

Riley, Susan. "A Migrant Mother." *Educational Leadership*, vol. 71, no. 3, 2013, pp. 92. *Academic Search Premier*, libproxy.sbcc.edu:2048 /login?url=https://search.ebscohost.com/login.aspx?direct=true&db =aph&AN=91736095&site=ehost-live&scope=site. Accessed 4 Feb. 2017.

Spirn, Anne Whiston. *Daring to Look: Dorothea Lange's Photographs and Reports from the Field*. U of Chicago P, 2009.

Zhang, Michael. "Iconic Photo Exposed: *Migrant Mother*." *PetaPixel.com*, 1 Aug. 2011, petapixel.com/2011/08/01/iconic-photo-exposed-migrant -mother/. Accessed 14 Apr. 2017.

A Brief Guide to Documentation

CITING YOUR SOURCES
SAMPLE CITATIONS

CITING YOUR SOURCES

Online Citation Help

Years ago, students needed a physical copy of a handbook to help them sift through the many types of citations required when writing academic essays. These days, though, while a handbook may still be useful, citation help is only a few keystrokes away.

The documentation style of the Modern Language Association (MLA) is widely available online, both through the libraries and writing centers of numerous colleges and universities, as well as on the websites of many major textbook publishers. (The MLA itself does not provide free online access to its style guide.)

The American Psychological Association, however, has its own website with examples of APA citations. It can be found at apastyle.org. The Chicago Style manual can also be accessed for free at the Chicago Manual of Style Online: chicagomanualofstyle.org.

Purdue's Online Writing Lab (owl.english.purdue.edu) features a complete listing of academic disciplines and the type of documentation style the discipline uses, with links to the discipline's main website as well as an online guide for each particular style. Moreover, many library databases, like Academic Search Premier, also include a fairly accurate feature for citing works from the database.

Therefore, while it's convenient to have the most common forms of citations in one place, as we do below for MLA documentation, all the information in this appendix can be found in authoritative form in many locations on the Internet.

Caveat

As helpful as the online world can be, even an established source like Academic Search Premier warns that students should "make any necessary corrections before using" a computer-generated citation in an essay, paying "special attention to personal names, capitalization, and dates." The cautionary note concludes: "Always consult your library resources for the exact formatting and punctuation guidelines."

If Academic Search Premier is capable of creating an incorrect reference, imagine how much more likely that is to happen on commercial citation generators like EasyBib.com. Yes, bibliographic management software is available—EndNote, ProCite, Reference Manager, Ref Works, and more—but it's always up to you, the author, to check your citation against an authoritative model.

Internal Citations

When citing your sources, you'll first reference them in the body of your essay (internal citations), then you'll provide fuller information at the end of the paper (in a Works Cited page). The internal citation is in parentheses; in other words, it is "parenthetical."

When you cite a source in your essay:

- Give only the information needed to identify the source, usually just the author's last name and a page number, if available.
- The parenthetical citation should precede the punctuation mark that concludes the sentence, usually a period.
- Place quotation marks immediately after the quotation and one blank space before the parenthetical citation.
- Place the parenthetical reference as close as possible to its source, usually at the end of a sentence.
- Information in the parenthesis should complement, not repeat, information given in the text. For example, if you include an author's name in the signal phrase, you don't need to repeat it in the parenthetical citation.
- Electronic and online sources are cited just like print resources in the body of your essay. If an online source lacks page numbers, omit numbers from the parenthetical references. If the source includes fixed page numbers or section numbering, such as numbering of paragraphs, cite the appropriate numbers.

Here are four examples of internal citations from the sample essays in Appendix I.

Print Source (with the author identified in the signal phrase)

As Shireen Khan Burki notes in "The Politics of *Zan* from Amanullah to Karzai," after the fall of the Taliban, initially "the government of the Islamic Republic of Afghanistan took major steps to restore the dignity of its female populace and improve their quality of life" (55).
—Emma Sandrolini, "Challenges for Women's Education in Afghanistan"

Print Source (with the author not identified in the signal phrase)

A recent study indicates that "reducing the prevalence of parental overweight and obesity would not only help preventing childhood obesity, but would in general lead to an improved health not only of the children, but also of their parents" (Cassell and Gleaves 6).
—Andrea Bottiani, "Childhood Obesity: Three Possible Solutions"

Online Source (with the author identified in the signal phrase)

Michael Zhang points out that Owens's thumb was originally shown "wrapped around the tent pole," but Lange subsequently used the tools of the day to erase this slight blemish.
—Eric Martinez, "What Makes a Great Photograph? Dorothea Lange's 'Migrant Mother'"

Online Source (with the author not identified in the signal phrase)

The withdrawal will also force European countries to pull out and give a yet another boost to the Taliban ("World Report 2013").
—Emma Sandrolini, "Challenges for Women's Education in Afghanistan"

Works Cited Page

References cited in the body of an academic essay must also appear at the end of the paper in a Works Cited page. The 8th edition of the MLA Handbook, published in 2016, made some significant changes from the 7th edition, particularly in regard to online sources. Nevertheless, citations for online sources provide essentially the same information as citations for print sources, including the author, the title, and what MLA calls the "container," the "larger whole in which the source is located."

Citing sources in a Works Cited page can feel rather complicated—often for good reason—but remember that documenting all your sources and doing so in the correct format demonstrates hard work and discipline on your part. Instructors know how time-consuming and tedious it can be to identify and use the proper citations, and they appreciate the difference between students who make a real, good faith effort and those who do a careless job.

When you are using MLA-style documentation, you will want to follow these guidelines:

- Arrange the entries in alphabetical order by authors' last names, or by title of the entry if there is no author.
- Capitalize the first word and all other principal words of the titles and subtitles of all works. (Don't capitalize minor words like articles, prepositions, or coordinating conjunctions.)
- Shorten the publisher's name: omit articles and business abbreviations (Co., Inc.), as well as descriptive words (Press, Publisher).
- Align the first line of the entry flush with the left margin, and indent all subsequent lines with a tab to form what is called a "hanging indent."

To illustrate these conventions, here, again, is the Works Cited page of Eric Martinez's "What Makes a Great Photograph? Dorothea Lange's 'Migrant Mother'":

Works Cited

Baird, Julia. "Seeing Dignity in Poverty." *Newsweek*, vol. 154, no. 20, 16 Nov. 2009, p. 30. *Academic Search Premier*, libproxy.sbcc.edu:2048 /login?url=https://search.ebscohost.com/login.aspx?direct=true&db =aph&AN=45137533&site=ehost-live&scope=site. Accessed 5 Feb. 2017.

Benfey, Christopher. "The Hunger Artists." *New Republic* vol. 240, no 22, 2 Dec. 2009, pp. 44–47. *Academic Search Premier*, libproxy.sbcc.edu:2048 /login?url=https://search.ebscohost.com/login.aspx?direct=true&db =aph&AN=45179697&site=ehost-live&scope=site. Accessed 5 Feb. 2017.

Curtis, James C. "Review of Kartin Beck Ohrn's *Dorothea Lange and the Documentary Tradition*." *Winterthur Portfolio*, vol.18, no. 1, 1983, pp. 116–17.

Gawthrop, Louis C. "Dorothea Lange and Visionary Change." *Society*, vol. 30, no. 5, 1993, pp. 64–67. *Academic Search Premier*, libproxy.sbcc .edu:2048/login?url=https://search.ebscohost.com/login .aspx?direct=true&db=aph&AN=9308317689&site=ehost-live&scope =site. Accessed 10 Feb. 2017.

Gordon, Linda. *Dorothea Lange: A Life Beyond Limits*. Norton, 2010.

Graham, Ed. "Top Photographers Answer, 'What Makes a Good Photograph?'" *Go See Write*, 8 July 2013, www.goseewrite.com/2013/07/top -photographers-answer-what-makes-a-good-photograph/. Accessed 2 Feb. 2017.

Lange, Dorothea. *Destitute Pea Pickers in California: Mother of Seven Children*, also known as *Migrant Mother*. 1936. National Archives, Washington, DC. *National Archives*, catalog.archives.gov/id/19626. Accessed 2 Feb. 2017.

Lucaites, John Louis, and Robert Hariman. "Visual Rhetoric, Photojournalism, and Democratic Public Culture." *Rhetoric Review*, vol. 20, no. 1–2, 2001, pp. 37–42.

Riley, Susan. "A Migrant Mother." *Educational Leadership*, vol. 71, no. 3, 2013, pp. 92. *Academic Search Premier*, libproxy.sbcc.edu:2048 /login?url=https://search.ebscohost.com/login.aspx?direct=true&db =aph&AN=91736095&site=ehost-live&scope=site. Accessed 4 Feb. 2017.

Spirn, Anne Whiston. *Daring to Look: Dorothea Lange's Photographs and Reports from the Field*. U of Chicago P, 2009.

Zhang, Michael. "Iconic Photo Exposed: *Migrant Mother*." *PetaPixel .com*, 1 Aug. 2011, petapixel.com/2011/08/01/iconic-photo-exposed -migrant-mother/. Accessed 14 Apr. 2017.

🚫 **Avoid This Common Error: Mistitling your Works Cited Page**. If you cite more than one work, it's "Works Cited," not "Work Cited" or "Works Citied" or "Bibliography." The phrase "Works Cited" should be in the same font and size as the rest of your document, centered, and just one double-spaced line above the beginning of your citations.

Identifying and Avoiding Plagiarism

Plagiarism is academic theft and refers to the use of another's words or ideas without proper attribution or credit. Credit must be given:

1. For every direct quotation.
2. When a work is paraphrased or summarized in whole or in part.
3. For information that is not common knowledge (that is, it appears in several sources about the subject).

In less formal language, plagiarism is using another's words or ideas as your own. This may range from "borrowing" a couple of sentences or ideas from someone else without giving them credit, to copying an entire paper from a book, the Internet, another person, etc.

In order to help them locate plagiarized papers, many instructors will require you to submit your essay to an online service like turnitin.com. Typically, a plagiarized essay results in a failing grade for the essay, and it may also result in a failing grade for the course. Plagiarism is also normally reported to your academic Dean, who will likely keep your name on file for the remainder of your time at your college or university.

Plagiarizing is bad for any number of reasons, but one of them is that your instructor generally *wants* you to research your topic. Therefore, unless you are quoting from an unreliable source or from one of the stock "paper mill" essays available online, you should take credit for locating, and then accurately quoting and acknowledging your secondary source.

Remember that plagiarizing material is the academic equivalent of committing a crime. Just as you will still be arrested for robbing a bank even if you claim you didn't know bank robbery was against the law, your instructor will penalize you for plagiarism whether or not you are aware you are doing it.

Avoid This Common Error: Unintentional plagiarism. Students who are caught plagiarizing will sometimes retreat to the position that *of course* they knew they were using someone else's material. *Anybody* would have known that. However, your professor will have had a range of experiences with plagiarizing students. Some students will have done so out of ignorance, but others will have done so with "malice aforethought," as attorneys say—an intentional desire to do no good. You can avoid inadvertent plagiarism by keeping careful track of which ideas and words are your own and which come from your sources.

Annotated Bibliography

Sometimes your instructor will require you to include an annotated bibliography along with your essay. An annotated bibliography looks very much like a Works Cited page, with a paragraph or two summarizing and evaluating each source. These sentences—the annotation—come immediately after the citation. As with a traditional MLA Works Cited page, you alphabetize your citations by the author's last name, or the first major word of the source if there is no author.

Here's a sample entry by Emma Sandrolini for her essay in Appendix I, "Challenges for Women's Education in Afghanistan":

Baker, Aryn, and Ali Safi. "The Girl Gap." *Time* 171.4 (2008): 40–43. Academic Search Premiere. Web. 18 Oct. 2013.

This periodical article focuses on women in Afghanistan and issues concerning their right to an education. It discusses ways in which Afghanistan has changed after the fall of the Taliban in 2001 and how the country has liberated women and given them a chance to attend school. However, the article notes that issues with Afghan cultural ideals regarding men and women still keep women from going to school.

You might be asked to write an annotated bibliography at any point during the composition process:

- *Before you begin writing your essay*, to ensure that you start writing with credible sources already in hand.
- *During the writing of your essay*, to help you keep track of the research you have done and to alert you to what you still need to learn.
- *After the writing of your essay*, to demonstrate to your instructor that your sources are credible and that you have used them appropriately.

SAMPLE CITATIONS

We'll conclude this appendix with the descriptions and examples of the most common types of entries on a Works Cited page.

Books

MLA end citations for entire books should include the following:

- Last Name, First Name of author(s) or editor(s).
- The complete title.
- Edition, if indicated,
- The shortened name of the publisher,
- Year of publication.

The Basic Format

Last name, First name. *Title of Book*. Publisher, Year of Publication.

A Book by One Author

Moore, Lorrie. *Bark: Stories*. Knopf, 2014.

Another Book by the Same Author

———. *Who Will Run the Frog Hospital?* Knopf, 1994.

A Book by Two Authors

Cook, Philip J., and Kristin A. Goss. *The Gun Debate: What Everyone Needs to Know.* Oxford UP, 2014.

A Book by Three or More Authors

Dyck, Arthur J., et al. *Life's Worth: The Case Against Assisted Suicide.* Eerdmans, 2002.

A Book by a "Corporate" Author

Toledo Museum of Art. *Toledo Treasures: Selections from the Toledo Museum of Art.* Hudson Hills, 1995.

Selections or Chapters in Edited Books or Anthologies

When you cite a book that includes work by many different authors, like a course reader or an anthology, follow this format. Scholarly books also often feature the work of numerous contributors. It's important to remember that for edited books and anthologies, the end citation begins with the last name of *the author who wrote the article or chapter,* not the editor of the book.

Citations for an essay or chapter in an edited book or compilation include the following:

- Last name, First Name of essay or chapter author(s).
- Essay or chapter title.
- Book title,
- Book editor(s) or compilers,
- The shortened name of the publisher,
- Year of publication,
- Inclusive page numbers of the cited piece.

An Article in a Book

Sommers, Nancy. "Responding to Student Writing." *On Writing Research: The Braddock Essays, 1975–1998,* edited by Lisa Ede, Bedford/St. Martins, 1999, pp. 122–29.

Articles in Journals, Magazines, and Newspapers

References to periodical articles include the following:

- Author(s).
- Article title.
- Publication title (journal, magazine, etc.),
- Volume and issue numbers,
- Publication date,
- The inclusive page numbers.

Volume and issue numbers should be indicated by the abbreviations "vol." and "no," as in the example below: vol. 45, no. 2.

A Journal Article

Vacante, Jeffrey. "The Posthumous Lives Of René Lévesque." *Journal of Canadian Studies*, vol. 45, no. 2, 2011, pp. 5–30.

A Magazine Article

Mead, Rebecca. "Musical Gold: Playing Strads for Fun and Profit." *The New Yorker*, 28 July 2014, pp. 32–39.

A Newspaper Article with Discontinuous Pages

Shaikin, Bill. "Angels Go with the Bundle Plan in Win." *Los Angeles Times*, 13 Aug. 2014, p. C1+.

Reference Books

As always, if the entry is signed, begin with the author's last name. If the entry is unsigned, alphabetize by the first major word of the entry's title.

An Encyclopedia Entry

Huang, Jeannie S. "Body Image." *Encyclopedia of Obesity*, vol. 2, Sage, 2008.

Audio Visual

Different types of visual and audio media require different information. For instance, you will need to know the location of a famous photograph or painting. Citations for films require you to know the director as well as the studio that produced the movie. Audio recordings require that you include not only the name of the artist and the work, but also the company that produced the recording. YouTube videos, which often include limited production information, are relatively easy to cite.

A Photograph

Lange, Dorothea. *Destitute Pea Pickers in California: Mother of Seven Children*, also known as *Migrant Mother*. 1936, National Archives, Washington, DC.

A Film or Movie

Deadpool. Directed by Tim Miller, 20th Century Fox, 2016.

A Sound Recording

West, Kanye. *Yeezus*, Rock-a-Fella/Def Jam, 2013.

A Specific Song on a Sound Recording

West, Kanye. "On Sight." *Yeezus*, Rock-a-Fella/Def Jam, 2013.

A YouTube Video

"Gangnam Style." *YouTube*. Web, uploaded by Psy, 15 July 2012, www .youtube.com/watch?v=9bZkp7q19f0&index=1&list=PLirAqAtl _h2r5g8xGajEwdXd3x1sZh8hC&ab_channel=officialpsy.

Online Sources

Citations of online sources should include the web address and the date the content was accessed. (Note that the web address should *not* include http:// or https://.) If the source was found through a password-protected database, like Academic Search Premier, be sure to identify the name of the database *and* provide either a "doi," a digital object identifier," or a "permalink" or "stable link" to the source.

If there is no date given for the last time an online source was updated, use "n.d." to indicate "no date." If no publisher is available, indicate that fact with the designation "n.p." (Remember, though, that if you cannot identify the publisher, you will probably want to avoid citing the source in your essay.)

Here are examples of a few of the most common online sources.

A Web Page

Art Gallery of Hamilton. "Visit AGH." *Art Gallery of Hamilton*, 2014,
  www.artgalleryofhamilton.com/va_index.php. Accessed 30 Aug. 2016.

An Entry in an Online Encyclopedia

"Wittgenstein, Ludwig." *Internet Encyclopedia of Philosophy*, 2013, www
  .iep.utm.edu/wittgens.

An Article in an Online Periodical

Waldman, Katy. "A Memorable Flight." *Slate*, 18 Aug. 2014, www.slate
  .com/articles/health_and_science/science/2014/08/plane_emergency
  _landing_psychology_study_people_with_ptsd_have_irrelevant.html.
  Accessed 28 Aug. 2106.

An Article in a Full-Text Journal Accessed from a Database

An article with a "digital object identifier," which can be found on the
article information page in the database.

Lyndon, Amy, Jennifer Bonds-Raacke, and Alyssa D. Cratty. "College Stu-
  dents' Facebook Stalking of Ex-Partners." *Cyberpsychology, Behavior
  & Social Networking*, vol. 14, no. 12, 2011, pp. 711–16. *Academic Search
  Premier*, doi: 10.1089/cyber.2010.0588. 7 June 2014.

An article *without* a "doi"; a "permalink," provided by the database, is used
instead of the full web address.

Wheeler, Thomas. "Facebook Fatalities: Students, Social Networking, and
  the First Amendment." *Pace Law Review*, vol. 31, no. 1, 2011, pp. 182–227.
  Academic Search Premier, libproxy.sbcc.edu:2048/login?url=https:
  //search.ebscohost.com/login.aspx?direct=true&db=aph&AN
  =60797301&site=ehost-live&scope=site. Accessed 29 May 2014.

An Online Book with Print Information

Emerson, Ralph Waldo. *Essays: First Series*. Phillips, Samson, 1850. *Google
  Books*, books.google.com/books?id=IERXAAAAYAAJ&dq=emerson
  %20essays&pg=PP9#v=onepage&q=emerson%20essays&f=false.

**Avoid This Common Error: Writing n.d. when the source *does*
include a publication date**. Citation generators often have trouble
locating dates of publication: check carefully before you settle for "n.d."

Permissions Acknowledgments

Text

Audrey Rock-Richardson. "Pay Your Own Way (Then Thank Mom)," from Newsweek, September 10, 2000. Reprinted with the permission of Audrey Rock.

Emma Sandrolini. "Challenges for Women's Education in Afghanistan." Reprinted with the permission of Emma Sandrolini.

Images

[Newtown image]
Photo copyright © Ron Haviv/VII/Redux

[Woman with gun image]
Photo copyright © Jan Mika

Index

From the Publisher

A name never says it all, but the word "Broadview" expresses a good deal of the philosophy behind our company. We are open to a broad range of academic approaches and political viewpoints. We pay attention to the broad impact book publishing and book printing has in the wider world; for some years now we have used 100% recycled paper for most titles. Our publishing program is internationally oriented and broad-ranging. Our individual titles often appeal to a broad readership too; many are of interest as much to general readers as to academics and students.

Founded in 1985, Broadview remains a fully independent company owned by its shareholders—not an imprint or subsidiary of a larger multinational.

For the most accurate information on our books (including information on pricing, editions, and formats) please visit our website at www.broadviewpress.com. Our print books and ebooks are also available for sale on our site.

broadview press
www.broadviewpress.com

The interior of this book is printed on 100% recycled paper.